First published in 2019 by Hachette Books Ireland
First published in paperback 2020

A CIP catalogue record for this title is available from the British Library.

ISBN 978 1 52937 845 0

Typeset in Sabon by redrattledesign.com

Printed and bound in Great Britain by Clays Ltd, Elcograf, S.p.A.

Hachette Books Ireland policy is to use papers that are natural, renewable
and recyclable products and made from wood grown in sustainable forests.
The logging and manufacturing processes are expected to conform to the
environmental regulations of the country of origin.

Hachette Books Ireland
8 Castlecourt Centre
Castleknock
Dublin 15, Ireland

A division of Hachette UK Ltd
Carmelite House, 50 Victoria Embankment, EC4Y 0DZ

www.hachettebooksireland.ie

If I Could Hold You Again

A true story about the devastating
consequences of bullying and
how one mother's grief
led her on a mission

COLLETTE WOLFE

With Brian Finnegan

HACHETTE
BOOKS
IRELAND

If I
Could
Hold You
Again

A true story about the devastating
consequences of bullying and
how one mother's grief
led her on a mission

Brian Finnegan is a writer and journalist living in Dublin. He is the author of two novels, *The Forced Redundancy Film Club* (2012) and *Knowing Me Knowing You* (2014), and has ghost-written several autobiographies for well-known Irish personalities. He edited GCN, Ireland's LGBT magazine, from 2003 to 2018 and over the past 20 years has been a regular contributor to many of the country's newspapers, magazines, radio and TV channels, writing and broadcasting mostly on LGBT politics and culture.

In memory of our beloved Leanne
Shining forever
Always in our hearts

There is a time for everything,
and a season for every activity under the heavens:
a time to be born and a time to die,
a time to plant and a time to uproot,
a time to kill and a time to heal,
a time to tear down and a time to build,
a time to weep and a time to laugh,
a time to mourn and a time to dance,
a time to scatter stones and a time to gather them,
a time to embrace and a time to refrain from embracing,
a time to search and a time to give up,
a time to keep and a time to throw away,
a time to tear and a time to mend,
a time to be silent and a time to speak,
a time to love and a time to hate,
a time for war and a time for peace.

– Ecclesiastes 3:1-8

Prologue

On 23 March 2007 I experienced the greatest loss a parent can ever know. It was the day my beautiful daughter, Leanne, left this world.

It was the day our lives changed for ever, a day that split my life in two, defined it by Before and After. Before that day I was an ordinary woman, raising three children with my husband the best I could in what I believed was a happy family. After it, nothing would be the same. My life would spiral out of control, until I was brought to another day that would change everything once more.

My daughter had just turned eighteen years old

when she took her own life. Her decision to go made me question everything I thought I knew. It turned me into a different person.

Leanne – the light of my life. I remember every detail of the day she left us as if it was only yesterday.

The Lanzarote breeze that was unusually high, on the island where myself and my husband Anthony had escaped for a winter getaway from our home in County Cork and the daily grind of work and family. It was a restless breeze that didn't let up, and it matched a feeling in my bones that day.

In many ways it was a day like any other in the resort, sunbathing on the beach, back to our room to freshen up for dinner at a restaurant in the town, a movie in the evening … except for the buzzing at the edges of my mind, a nervy feeling that wouldn't shift.

A mother's intuition? I sometimes wonder what we know deep down in our bones.

All parents worry. It's like this secret contract you sign the moment your first child is born: *I will worry about you, almost as much as I love you.* And I did worry for Leanne – she was a teenager, after all, and experienced all of the ups and downs that involves. But we were close. She talked to me. We had our ups and downs, too – we were both sparky. But she knew I had her back. I always had her back.

With the wind blowing on the beach, it was hard to relax, so I suggested to Anthony we'd go for dinner earlier than usual. Normally we'd have a shower after the beach and get cleaned up before heading out, but this time we went straight to the restaurant. I remember we had the most beautiful meal, and we ate our fill. I was after losing a load of weight over the past couple of years, and it was a miracle that I'd kept it off. But we were on holidays, our first without any of the children, and I was treating myself.

After the restaurant we went home to watch a movie, picking up some munchies at the supermarket along the way. Though I don't recall what the movie was, I remember that before it started I looked at Anthony and thought about the fierce admiration I had for him: what a good husband and father he'd always been. For years, I suppose, I'd never realised how much I loved him. We got engaged, we got married, we had children, we made a life together, yet love wasn't something I really thought about when it came to us.

But here we were, on holidays together after so many years and so many huge ups and downs, and everything seemed to have fallen into place. Our children were doing well. They weren't saints – Anthony, Triona and Leanne – far from it. But they were well-adjusted kids. We'd brought them up in a home where they didn't have to live in fear, and I felt proud of the work we'd done with them. Leanne was going to be heading off to college soon, and then they'd all have flown the nest. I felt I had done nothing much worthwhile with my own life, but at least with my children, I thought, *I was a part of that.*

I'd love to say I was contemplating all this after a bottle of wine, but we were both stone-cold sober. I looked at my husband and said, 'Anthony, you're my best friend and I love you.'

There was no immediate answer.

'Well?' I asked, getting impatient.

'Right back at you,' Anthony replied, and I burst out laughing. He's a man of few words, my husband.

We watched the movie and had our munchies, and then we went to bed early. I was exhausted from the beach and the sun and the food, and I dropped off fairly fast.

Somewhere in the middle of my sleep I heard a phone ringing. It sounded like it was coming from far away.

Anthony got out of the bed to answer it and I sat up. There was no hello or anything, just Anthony saying, 'What are you talking about?'

I'd gotten out of bed, too, and was trying to get closer to hear what was going on.

'It's Leanne, Dad,' I heard my son Anthony saying on the phone.

In the background I could hear another voice saying, 'Tell them, you have to tell them.'

My whole insides were churning. I knew something terrible was coming, like a train speeding down a track.

'Leanne's gone,' my son said.

'Gone where?' said my husband.

'Leanne is dead,' said my son.

With those words, what I can only describe as a journey into Hell began.

If I could stand beside the woman in that hotel room in Lanzarote that night, as she clutched on to her husband's arm and heard her son tell them that their daughter had taken her own life, I'd say to her, 'You have to go on this journey.'

Even though she went on it kicking and screaming, I'd tell her, 'You have to go through this Hell to come out the other end.'

I would say to that woman, standing in that hotel room, as her husband began to scream, 'You will feel guilt that will bring you to the brink of ending your own life. You will think you were the worst kind of mother, a mother whose child chose to die. But you were a good mother. You gave the biggest gift to your children. You gave them love.'

I'd tell that woman that one day she will dance again, that she will sing, but it will be a different song and a different dance. I would say to her, 'You have no idea that from this journey into Hell you will come to experience a little bit of Heaven.'

Soon I would learn the reasons why my daughter had taken an overdose, why she'd laboured through her last breaths over the course of that long day in her bedroom, while my husband and I lay on a windswept beach, and filled our faces in a restaurant, and ate munchies, laughing and watching a movie whose name I can't remember. I'd learn Leanne's terrible secrets.

When I got the news that my daughter had committed suicide, I immediately took control. I tried to look after my husband; I tried to look after my other two children; I tried to hold their world together. But inside I was right back to being an eight-year-old child again. My own world was broken, everything was gone and nothing could be trusted.

Looking back I shouldn't have been surprised that Leanne had kept secrets, that she'd hidden her torment. Secrets and torment had been in my blood since I was that eight-year-old little girl, from the day another journey into Hell began.

1

It began with a story about a little white mouse.

The man took me aside and whispered that he'd found a little white mouse upstairs in the bedroom.

A little white mouse! I was all excited. He told me I might be able to keep it as a pet. 'Come on and I'll show you,' he said, so I followed him.

When we got upstairs, he closed the bedroom door. There was a big walk-in cupboard and he told me the mouse was in there.

I went in and searched through the gloom for the little white mouse, but there was no sign of it.

'I can't find it,' I said, peeping out of the cupboard.

Then he told me to get onto the bed.

I did what I was told, and that was the moment my childhood ended.

I was one of eleven children. There were so many of us, I was in the second generation. Born in 1961, I was fourth from the youngest. We lived in Ballyphehane, on the southside of Cork, a nice place with a salt-of-the-earth community, and we were seen as a good, respectable family.

This was more to do with my mam than my dad. Her home was absolutely spotless and we were always well turned out. Dinner would be cooked for all of us at the same time every day. She wasn't the greatest cook – to be honest, she was a disaster – but she put a meal on the table every day without fail. Our father would balance a plank of wood on two chairs at either end to make a bench each side of the table, and we'd all sit down and eat together.

We might have had nothing, but my mam always wanted the best for us. She even got us elocution lessons.

Christened Anne McCarthy, she was known to all as Annie. She was only six years of age when her own mam died and seven when her dad went the same way. A neighbour took her in and loved her, but she was an elderly woman and when she passed away little Annie went to her mother's stepsister, Mary. There was nobody else could take her.

Mary's husband didn't treat my mam well. He was very good to his own children, but I suppose she wasn't his child. I reckon things happened in that house that she never spoke about.

She never brought her past into her own home. My mam's family came first. Her children would be always looked after, but she wouldn't buy herself a coat. She was very grateful for what she had, no matter what little it was.

My father was a fierce drinker, so she would have been the one with the burden of providing for all us children. Mam worked in St Finbarr's hospital as a cleaner on night shifts, and when she came home she'd sleep for maybe two or three hours only, before getting up to have us ready and out for school.

My dad could be a violent man. I don't remember him beating her, but the older girls do. I can remember the shouting, though, and my sister running down the stairs and yelling at him, 'Get away from my mam!'

In later years I'd ask her, 'Why didn't you leave him?' and Mam would reply, 'But look what he gave me, all my children.'

Dad was a big, intimidating man, and it didn't come out well for you if you got on the wrong side of him, which was an easy thing to do. Even when he died at the age of seventy-two, he was eighteen stone, but his weight was more in his height than his width. Beside Dad, my mam was a tiny little thing, but there was a part of her that was fearless when it came to him.

Once when he was on the drink mightily and it was coming up to pay day, Mam knew she wasn't going to see his wages, so she decided to get my brother to go up to the phone in the local shop and call the pub for him – we had no phone at that time.

'Say it's an anonymous call and that his wife Annie Kearney is just after being taken out of the river,' she told him.

My dad was actually carried in the door by his friends, hysterically bawling that our mother had drowned. And there she was, sitting at the kitchen table, waiting for him.

'I got a terrible phone call,' he cried. 'They said you'd been dragged out of the river.'

Mam threw her eyes up to Heaven. 'It was one of your stupid, drunken friends that played that trick,' she said.

She'd gotten him home, though. She'd gotten her money.

When he was sober my dad had a very generous side to him. I just think he was very broken and damaged. His name was John Kearney and he came from the Middle Parish in Cork, which was a very rough area back when he was a boy. His mother let him go into an industrial home when he was very young, when she could have avoided it. Like my mam didn't speak of her past, my father never mentioned his time in there.

Mam often said to us, 'God only knows what happened to him.'

He worked in construction when I was younger, and later on oil rigs. His wages might often have been spent buying rounds of drink for everyone in the pub, instead of feeding his children, but he was very handy at home. He could build anything and we had a lovely house.

As I said, there were two generations of children. The older ones were Martin, Annabelle, Christine, Noely, Veronica, John and Frances. I was the oldest of the younger gang, and after me there was Rosarie, Loretta and Michael.

The four of us young ones were very tight-knit, and of the older ones, I was especially close to Frances. We were forever up to mischief. I remember we'd tie the string to the knocker of the house across the road from us, then bring it across to ours. We'd pull the string and leave it settle on the ground, and when the neighbours came out to answer their door, they wouldn't know what was going on. One night they traced the string, and we were desperately trying to cut it, because they'd have come and told our mam and we'd have been murdered.

Dad was very, very strict. If somebody did something wrong and he got wind of it, they'd be given lashes of the belt. We'd be in our bedroom on those occasions, the four of us huddled in the one bed, waiting for him to come up. Our biggest dread would be if he made one of us get out and make the bed, because you knew you were going to get the belt then, and it would be the buckle part. We'd hear his footsteps on the stairs and we'd be terrified.

Somehow I didn't get into trouble as much as the rest of them. I was invisible in a way because the others, Loretta and Michael mostly, got into such terrible mischief. I didn't like the anxiety, the thought of Dad coming up the stairs, the waiting for his belt. When he got into the room, though, I'd show no fear, even though I'd be petrified. I've brought that through life with me. I could be literally terrified but I'd cover it up and it helped make me invisible.

I think maybe it was my invisibility that singled me out for the story about the little white mouse and what happened afterwards. Because a child who can't be seen can't tell.

2

The abuse started off slowly, for the first couple of days. He did things to me; he made me do things to him. After that it became more extreme.

This man, who has since passed away, was someone who had our family's trust, and who had access to our home. He knew how to pick his opportunities when he could do his evil bidding without being caught. He said that if I told anybody, they wouldn't believe me and that he'd beat the living daylights out of me. After he was finished, he'd call me a dirty bitch. He filled my head with lies until I came to believe it was my fault, that I'd made him do it.

I went from a child to an adult overnight, so much so that I have barely any memories of the years beforehand. I had been an outgoing, trusting child, but now I became withdrawn and quiet. I learned not to trust anyone.

At first I was very confused, because I didn't know what was actually happening. I was a completely innocent child – I didn't even know what sex was, let alone rape.

All I knew was that I hated what was happening. It was painful. It made me feel dirty, a feeling that soon came to be with me all the time. I felt trapped, too, and lonely – so lonely.

I think the sense of shame was worse than the abuse. Even in the years after it had all ended, the shame ate away at my insides. I knew things I shouldn't have known, I'd done things no child should ever do, and I hadn't done anything to stop it.

Fear took over my life. I felt shrouded in darkness. If you had asked me as a young adult if I believed in the devil, I would have said yes, but if you'd asked me whether God existed, I would have said no, because God had disappeared for me. The nuns taught us about God in school, but my schooldays were filled with a gnawing kind of terror. Any chance that man had, he was always waiting for me, always finding ways to get me alone.

After school, I'd stand alone on the corner of my

street. There'd be other children out playing, laughing and riding their bicycles. I couldn't ride a bike, and somehow this became part of my shame. I somehow believed it was because I wasn't as good as other children. They looked like they had so much freedom, flying up and down the street. But that freedom wasn't for me because I wasn't like them. I was a 'dirty bitch'. I didn't deserve to know how to ride a bike, to know that freedom and fun.

Inside I was alone, isolated and apart, and at the same time I was terrified of being alone. I tried to stay around other people all the time, but he would always find a way to get me on my own. Always.

If you looked at this man, you would never have thought in a million years that he could have done what he did to me. He was the life and soul of the party. Women loved him, my family loved him. He had this kind of aura about him that people were drawn to. There'd be a different girl on his arm every weekend.

I remember thinking the abuse was never going to end. Later, when I had my own children, I would look at them and marvel at their innocence. It wasn't a feeling I had known from a young age, and even as an adult, it was a long time before I could see my childhood self that way. Like every victim of abuse who stays silent, my abuser had done a good job of brain-washing me. I felt responsible.

The abuse went on for over three years. I didn't

reach out to anyone, and all that time I stayed silent. I couldn't bring myself to tell my sisters, not even Frances, who I was so close to. It was my shameful secret that couldn't be shared, and with it I learned to keep a lot of other shameful secrets, something that stayed with me as I grew up. For ten years after we got married, my own husband never knew that I couldn't read or write. Just as I learned to keep the abuse, which had been right under everyone's noses, a secret, I was able to pass with Anthony as a woman who could read and write.

I grew up thinking there was something wrong with me. I grew up telling myself I was a bad person, that I did not deserve happiness. For decades after the abuse had ended, I would have dreams of it being repeated. I'd wake up and vomit. I've learned since then that these dreams are normal for survivors of sexual abuse, but at the time it only added to the shame that was coiled deep inside me. I'd be thinking, *What kind of human being am I*? I'd be upset for weeks after the dream, afraid of going to sleep, afraid of the dark.

The abuse went on until I was eleven and ended as suddenly as it began. Maybe I'd grown too old for him and he'd lost interest in me. All I know is that I was left with a burden of guilt that lasted well into my adult life, and a fear and distrust of the world that would come to prove itself again very soon.

3

My abuser trained me well in the art of keeping secrets. He also trained me to hate myself. I often wonder if I hadn't been trapped in secrecy and self-loathing, if I'd learned to be open and unashamed about what had happened to me, whether my daughter would have learned not to keep the secrets she did. We thought Leanne was 'model material'. She was a natural beauty and she was smart as a whip. But other people had trained her to hate herself.

When we found her diaries, on the day of her funeral, we discovered a girl who wrote things like 'I'm nothing. I'm nobody.'

Maybe it's an Irish thing. You don't wash your dirty linen in public. You don't upset the apple cart. My husband hardly says a word about his own childhood. Even now, when his sister tells me stories about how his mam treated him, I'm shocked.

I met Anthony when I was fifteen, at a disco. I'd left school two years earlier, having slipped through the cracks. I lasted just a couple of months in secondary school. I was filled with fear going there because I couldn't write or spell or read. But I was kind of passed over, the way I had been by the nuns in primary because I wasn't from a well-off family and I had difficulties learning.

The decision to leave was mine, but the school didn't really have an interest in me. I wasn't bringing anything to it, and I wasn't learning anything, so if you got a job, they were more than happy to let you go.

My first job was in a chicken factory for ten pounds a week. I'd get the bus at six in the morning and work until six in the evening. I felt more in control because I was earning, but I hated the place. I was only a child, when you think about it, working with all these older women, and they treated me and my friend, who was the same age, very badly, giving us the awful jobs. To this day my stomach turns if I think about cleaning out chickens.

When I was fifteen I got a job in Byrne's meat-processing factory in Ballincollig. My dad knew one of the foremen there, and he got me in. My sister Frances worked there too. I liked Byrne's, and I was good at the work. My only problem was with deliveries, which involved writing. I'd run to Frances and she'd write down what I had to write on my hand or a bit of paper, and I'd go back and copy it into the delivery form.

By day I wore the factory uniform and by night I was a jeans and Doc Martens girl. I loved the Bay City Rollers and I'd have a tartan strip sewn down the side of my Wranglers, the way all their fans did. My younger sister Rosarie was a girly girl. She just loved wearing dresses. I'd say to her, 'You're mad to wear those dresses. They make you a target, girl.'

That was really how I felt about myself. I was a target, so I had to cover up the best I could. I put this big front on. I'd make everything into a joke so that nobody would see the real me. They wouldn't clock that I was like a scared child, that I was dirty.

The abuse was always there, beneath the surface. I was very wary, always on the watch when men were around, constantly on the lookout for something that didn't seem right.

The disco was in Cork city centre and it was called the Stardust. It had UV lights on the dance-floor, and all the girls wore white tights so their legs would glow. On the night I met Anthony, I was a bit more girly than usual, wearing a skirt with the obligatory white tights.

Two fellas came over to my friend Mary and me to ask if we'd like a dance. Anthony was one of them.

While we were dancing he chatted away. He was very friendly and I knew from the start there was a decent streak in him. When the disco was finished he asked if he could walk me home. It was a fair distance from the city centre to Ballyphehane, but I told him he could.

When we got as far as the corner of my street I stopped. I looked at him and said, 'If you're after coming all the way up here for something, you're not getting it.'

He said he had no plans to try anything at all.

'I was just clearing that up,' I told him.

We started dating. I remember going to the cinema with him for the first time, all excited that I was going to the pictures with a fella.

I really liked him, and liked being with him, and I knew he liked me. It was the first time I felt safe with somebody, that I didn't feel vulnerable. He wore Ben Sherman shirts and Levi's, and although he wasn't tall, he held himself well. I didn't fully realise what I had in Anthony for many years, not until the months before my sister Frances died and I saw what he did for her through her sickness. Back at the beginning, I took him for granted.

We continued dating for about two years, going to the pictures, going to dances, sitting in watching telly. Sex didn't come into the equation. Then one day my friend Liz said to me, 'You're far too young to be so serious with a fella. There's plenty more fish in the sea.'

I was very young, it's true, very young and immature. I listened to her and that night, I said to Anthony, 'I want a break.'

'Do you, now?' he replied. 'Well, you can have a break for the rest of your life.'

A few days later, Liz asked him out! She came into work one morning with a love bite on her neck and I was thinking, *She's having sex with him. He's definitely going to stay with her, because he was getting nothing from me.*

I fancied another fella I'd seen around the place, so that took my mind off it a bit. This guy had come home from England and he had an air of glamour about him. I liked his accent – it seemed like he had a bit of class.

It turned out he didn't have any class at all. In fact he was dangerous. It took a Christmas night out and the first two glasses of lager I ever drank to put me in a position I would normally have been watching out for, like a hawk.

4

Young people nowadays seem to drink much more than we did in my day. We discovered from Leanne's diaries that she'd go out with a gang of girls and the lot of them would get so drunk on vodka they'd be hardly able to stand up.

By the age of seventeen, alcohol hadn't passed my lips. I never usually went out to parties much, but my friend Catherine fancied a guy called Dan from the factory, and she persuaded me to come to one where she knew he'd be. I fancied your man who was home from England, who was also likely to be there so we were both in high spirits.

I had two glasses of Heineken, and they went straight to my head. The fella home from England asked me if I wanted to go for a walk with him. Catherine was going for a walk with Dan, so I laughed and said yes. They went one way, and we went the other, and when we got to an isolated little place, we started kissing.

It got heated very quickly. His hands were everywhere and I began to feel scared. I started telling him, 'No,' but he kept going.

The more I tried to stop him, the more forceful he got. I pushed him hard in his chest and he fell back, shouting something at me. I ran away in a blind panic.

I got to a tennis court, with a net across it, and that was what stopped me. I couldn't get past it before he caught up with me.

He grabbed me by the hair and flung me on the ground. I don't remember much of what happened after that. It's still a blank in my mind, the way much of my childhood is completely gone.

What I do remember is that, when it was over, he acted as if nothing had happened, as if we'd had a good time. He said he wasn't worried about me being pregnant because he hadn't come inside me.

I didn't realise as he was telling me this that I was disfigured. I'd blocked out the terrible beating he'd given me.

'Come on, I'll get you home,' he said, as if it was a normal night out. I only wanted to get away from him, so I stumbled away and he let me go.

I was out on the street in Ballincollig and a bus came along. I waved it down. I was covered in blood, so God knows what the driver thought as I paid my fare. He didn't say anything to me.

I got off at the wrong stop, in town, so I ended up walking for a good half-hour before I got home. I didn't know I had only one boot on. My pants and legs were sopping, because I'd wet myself. There were about a million and one things going through my head as I walked, and at the same time I was completely dazed and numb.

Part of me thought I'd done something to encourage it. Why did I go for a walk with him? Why, when I knew what could happen?

When I got to our house, my mam opened the door and she knew immediately what had happened. She grabbed me in and pandemonium broke out.

I remember she ran a bath for me. There was only a few inches of water in it and the rest was Dettol. I thought she was afraid I was after getting something, but what I couldn't see was the state of my face, or the fact that chunks of my hair had been torn out. I couldn't feel any pain at all.

My mam called the guards and they came to the house. They took away all the clothes I'd been wearing, and they asked a lot of questions, which I don't remember answering. There was a female guard. She wasn't kind, like you might expect of a woman. There was no sympathy, and I felt as if I'd done wrong.

That night, I woke up screaming. I'd suffered from nightmares before, but this one was ten times worse. For some reason, I always thought it was my older sister Frances who looked after me, but it was Loretta, who was only a child at the time. She must have fallen asleep sitting up, with me in her arms, because when I woke up she was holding me, telling me it was okay.

He'd given me such a beating that it was six weeks before I could go back to work. The guards tried to do an investigation, but my rapist had been shipped back to England by his parents. They got him out of the country within twenty-four hours, and I was glad of it because I didn't have to face him.

The guards were involved, so my biggest fear came true. My rape was known about all over Cork. I stayed at home, in the front room, and I was so ashamed I thought I'd never go out again.

Talk got back to the house. Some were saying I deserved it. Some were saying it was all lies, that I had ruined a boy's reputation and life. A rumour started up that I was pregnant.

The worst part of it was my abuser knowing. I still saw him regularly, and I could see he was gloating, telling me with his smile that I'd got what I deserved. It made me sick to my stomach.

A week and a half after the rape I was sitting inside the front room in my dressing gown when there was a knock at the front door. My heart leaped into my mouth, but when my mam opened the door, there was Anthony.

He had flowers in his arms for me, a big bunch of red roses.

5

I've said before that Anthony is a quiet man. He's a steady man too, always there, always taking care of things in the background. His relationship with Leanne was very close. She relied on his calm strength. I remember once, when she'd forgotten her lunch at school and I was at work, he drove ten miles from the building site he was working on to bring her something to eat.

That was what was so hard to take in about her suicide, the fact that she didn't come to either of us for help, not to me, who would stand up for her to anyone, not to her father, who was always there for her – a constant, gentle, kind support.

After my rape, Anthony didn't ask a single question. He just gave me the flowers and sat in the room with me silently, as if he was softly saying, 'I'm here for you.'

Even after we got married, he never asked. I was still waiting for the awkward queries. *Why did you go for a walk with him? What were you doing before he raped you?* For a while, I wouldn't even tell Anthony that I'd had two glasses of Heineken.

But that day we didn't get back together. We became more like good friends. I thought, *Why would he want to make up with me?* I felt as though I'd been damaged goods already, that the rape was just more on top of it. How could I be worthy of a man like him?

I didn't realise that Anthony loved me. How could I? I didn't even know what love was. To me the idea of love between a man and a woman was something horrendous, because love was sex. For now, it would have to be friendship. I guess, looking back, even if I didn't know it, I was learning to trust – for the first time.

A couple of days later Anthony called back to the house. And then he called again. I liked to see him coming. He didn't wear his heart on his sleeve. Even the flowers were a big gesture for him because he was a man's man.

After six weeks my mam insisted that I go back to work. She said I'd done nothing wrong and that I had to face the world again. She was right, but it was very hard to walk into that factory with my head held up. The morning I went back, I got sick before I left the house.

I remember thinking, *They're waiting to see if I'm pregnant*. And then thinking, *Maybe I am pregnant*. Because although he'd said he'd pulled out before he ejaculated, how was I to know he was telling the truth?

I got obsessed with worry that I was pregnant. I knew I wouldn't be able to keep it a secret. Everyone would know that this baby was a rape baby. They wouldn't ever see it as anything else. I knew I would have loved the baby, because it had no part in the rape. I started praying to God, 'Please, don't let me be pregnant,' but the more I prayed the more convinced I became that I was.

I made a plan that if a pregnancy was confirmed, I'd go to England and I'd rear the child there, because Ireland was too small a place where everybody knew your business.

It turned out I wasn't pregnant, and I was so relieved. But I still had to face the fact that I couldn't keep my rape a secret.

It wasn't like the sexual abuse, where I could hide. It was out: people talked and gave me funny looks. For the first while at work there were comments, words like 'slut' and 'asking for it'. They'd be said just loud enough for me to hear.

I didn't say anything. I kept my head down and got on with my work. I hated arguments, I hated confrontation, and the part of me that felt it was my own fault agreed with those horrible words.

I was glad my rapist had done a runner because I couldn't have borne going to court, with everybody looking at me and barristers asking questions. *Why did you go for a walk with him? How many drinks did you have?*

I knew it would be very hard to prove he raped me. I was afraid, too, of other things coming out in court. I knew that fear was irrational, but it was there nonetheless. The court case would have gone on and on, and I don't know if I'd have had the mental strength to cope. I was on the edge as it was. I felt that I was crumbling, barely holding myself together.

Strangely, I didn't hate the rapist. Somewhere inside, maybe I thought I deserved what he'd done to me. The seeds of self-hatred sown by my abuser were buried deep.

After a couple of weeks the talk at work died down. I was yesterday's news, and I was glad of it.

Anthony kept calling to the house and eventually we slipped into a pattern and started dating once more. He never looked for anything or tried anything on with me. We kissed and cuddled, of course, but that was about as far as it went. I got very comfortable with him again, going along the way we were.

He didn't ask me to marry him directly. We were passing by Keane's jeweller's one day and he stopped to look at the display of rings in the window. 'What do you think?' was all he said.

There was no going down on one knee. If he had, I would have been in a state of shock. We just agreed to get engaged. We went in on a Saturday, picked out the ring and had a meal afterwards.

We made a plan between the two of us that on the night of our engagement party we would sleep together.

We had a really big celebration in the Haven bar, with all our friends and families there. Towards the end of the party I was starting to get cold feet, not because of the sex but because I was deathly afraid that somebody might see us going into the hotel. From bitter experience, I knew that people talked. I'd been called a slut.

When we got as far as the hotel, I said, 'I can't do it, Anthony.'

He had been on a high about the whole endeavour, so he was gutted. We ended up having a big fight, standing on a bridge and yelling at each other. I took off the ring and flung it at him. Luckily it didn't end up in the Lee.

It was all off, but we ended up going home together anyway. I picked the ring up and put it back on.

I confided in a friend of mine that I hadn't been able to go through with the night in the hotel. She was doing a strong line with a fella, and she said, 'We'll go to a place, the four of us. Somewhere we won't be seen.'

We all booked into a bed-and-breakfast on the Lower Road. It was the worst of the worst. I'd say there were even fleas in the beds, but it served its purpose because I felt no one we knew would be around.

The sex wasn't as bad as I'd imagined it would be. It wasn't something that would blow you away, but when it was over the ice was broken. After that we'd go away to Killarney or Dublin every so often and book a hotel.

Things got easier and nicer, but I still found it very hard to trust. I was very much on my guard for a long time throughout my marriage, still afraid of being hurt.

We didn't take any precautions. You couldn't get precautions at the time in Ireland anyway. So, a couple of months before our big day, I discovered I was pregnant. It was 1980 and pregnancies outside marriage were still taboo, but I was over the moon and Anthony was ecstatic. Our wedding plans took second place to the excitement we felt at being prospective parents.

As it turned out, we needn't have been excited about the wedding anyway. From the first moment of that special day, we had an almighty calamity on our hands.

6

People look forward to their weddings; I just wanted to get mine over and done with. There was a chance that my abuser might be there. By rights, he shouldn't have been invited, but I was afraid to cause trouble, and it was natural that he'd get an invitation.

Then there was Anthony's mother. I was afraid of her, and she'd made it long clear she didn't have much time for me. She thought I was too uppity, too posh, although our family had nothing. My father knew Mrs Wolfe before I met Anthony, and that meant she frequented the hard drinkers' pubs.

She was separated from Anthony's father and didn't want him to be at the wedding. But I felt he couldn't be left out. Although he was troubled and suffered from depression, he was a nice man. On the morning of the wedding, Anthony went up to where he lived to shave him and put on his suit.

My youngest sister Loretta was my matron of honour and my older sister Frances was bridesmaid, and her firstborn, Clifford, the pageboy. Frances was due at our house with them at eight in the morning, but there was no sign of her. Nor was there at nine, or ten, or eleven. Of course she'd slept in, even though the night before I'd warned her she'd better set a hundred alarms. She was an awful one for sleeping late, Frances. An earthquake couldn't have woken her some mornings.

We had no phone in the house to call her and time was marching on. The wedding was at noon and by a quarter to, my father was like a lunatic, yelling, 'We have to get to the church now!'

My sister Annabelle was a bit calmer, but she said, 'You have to go, Collette.'

'I'm not going without Frances,' I replied, folding my arms in my big white wedding dress.

When she arrived at a quarter past, she was genuinely sorry. She'd slept it out. She couldn't get a taxi and never even got to the hairdresser. By the time we got to the church it was nearly one o'clock.

Dad, who had gone ahead, was waiting at the church

door to walk me down the aisle. 'Anthony's like a bear in there,' he muttered.

When I finally got to the altar the priest was looking at Anthony's thundering expression and I could see him thinking, *This is going to be some show.*

To break the tension, he said, 'What's another year?'

Anthony looked at me and said, 'You can eff off.'

I bit my lip to stop myself answering back. I knew he was ready to walk, and I'd be left at the altar if I said anything. I knew he'd be sorry tomorrow if he did.

We got married, said the words about in sickness and in health, exchanged rings, the whole lot, without even looking at each other. When we got out of the church and into the car, Anthony barked at me, 'Don't even try to give me an excuse.'

He still didn't know what had happened until Frances sat him down months later and told him she was the reason I was late. He'd felt I was making a fool of him, leaving him waiting. His brothers had been winding him up in the church, saying, 'If she's starting this way, what's she going to be like a couple of months down the road?'

At the reception, we barely talked. We must have danced the first dance together, but I can't remember. 'This is supposed to be the most wonderful day of my life,' I told Frances, as my new husband got up to sing.

As he started into 'Tie a Yellow Ribbon Round the

Ole Oak Tree' I thought, *He's only married a few hours and he already thinks he's doing time.*

Then he sang a song to his mother, who hadn't stopped scowling at me since the moment I'd arrived at the church.

I was afraid Mrs Wolfe would say something awful about me to my parents. Mam was a lady, she wouldn't say anything in reply, but you could be sure my dad would tell her where to go.

Oh, my God, they'll be talking about this wedding for the next twenty years, I was thinking. The whole thing felt like it would never end.

Our honeymoon was a few days in Dublin. We argued all the way there on the train and more when we got to our hotel. Anthony mellowed after about twenty-four hours, but I couldn't bring up the subject, or tell him why I was late, because it would be back to arguing and fighting.

We calmed down, went out for meals, he had his couple of pints, but it wasn't what you might call a beginning that boded well for the future.

We moved into a tiny downstairs flat in Blackrock, only one room with a kitchenette. We made it our own little home.

Anthony was a hard worker and a good provider, but he liked to go for a pint or two with the lads after work. This was like waving a red rag at a bull when it came to me. I didn't want to end up like my mam, with my dad out getting plastered all the time. I'd expected a whole different thing from marriage, roses on a Friday, a bit of romance. I wasn't long getting a reality check. We argued so much that every weekend I'd pack my bags and go home or to stay with Frances.

Our son, Anthony junior, was born a couple of weeks before Easter in 1981. The elder Anthony never made it to the birth because he was working on a site and we couldn't contact him there. When I went into labour, my mam brought me into the hospital.

The midwife, Lucy, was very abrupt, but she was good at her job. When we arrived, I felt that the baby was going to be born soon.

'How many children do you have?' she asked.

'This is my first,' I told her, and she said I'd be a long time. Mam had run off to find Anthony and I was sitting there by myself, resisting the urge to push because Lucy had told me not to.

When she came back into the room, I said, as politely as I could, 'Excuse me, I think I want to have the baby now.'

When Lucy examined me, she said, 'Oh, my God, the head is already out!'

Little Anthony was born fairly fast after that.

I remember bringing him out in the most beautiful sunshine when we left the hospital, full of the joys of spring. Unfortunately, that was the end of the joys. I didn't get what you'd call a quiet little baby. He never stopped crying and I was sure it was my fault, that I was doing something wrong. No matter what I did, I couldn't comfort him. I'd think he was crying with hunger so I'd give him a bottle, and that would only make him worse.

The baby never slept at night and I went beyond exhaustion. When Anthony came in from work, I'd be like a demon and we'd fight like cats and dogs.

'Happy little family,' he'd say to me sarcastically, and out would come my bag and the baby's bag. I'd pack them up and storm out, off home again.

We were so young, Anthony and I, barely out of our teens and desperately trying to be grown-ups. It wasn't working out too well.

7

Nobody told me how to be a mother. Let's face it, no one does. The biggest job you'll ever take on, and you're just expected to row in and do it, as my mother had and her mother before her. I made mistakes, as all parents do, and this would haunt me in the months and years following Leanne's death. What terrible things had I done wrong? How was I to blame?

My sense of wrongdoing, of somehow not being a good enough mother, was with me from the start. I relate it back to when I was a child and the feelings I had around not being able to ride a bike. The shame I felt. The deep-seated belief that I didn't deserve good things because I was a bad person.

I won't lie. There were times when I felt like throwing the Moses basket, with Ant in it, out the window. I wrote in his baby book that his actual first smile came when he was eight months old. There were moments when his little stomach gave him a rest and he'd quiet down, and I'd marvel at how beautiful he was, my heart full of the love that only the parent of a firstborn can know, but there were times when he had me at my wits' end.

Then he suddenly settled, going from one extreme to the other overnight. He got so quiet that I'd check him to see was he still alive. Ant didn't give me an ounce of trouble from that day on, never raised his voice. He's still the same quiet lad, married now with his own children.

If I said no, to Ant, he took me at my word. Triona, who came along two and half years later, was a different kettle of fish. She didn't comprehend the word 'no'.

She was born on 22 September 1983, two weeks overdue. When I got pregnant with her I was a size ten, but by the time she was born I'd gone up to fourteen stone. We'd had a heatwave the previous summer and I lived on Fanta and Lion bars. I was so overweight you wouldn't have known I was pregnant.

Triona had to be nearly dragged out – it was like she didn't want to be born. For all the pain, I was overjoyed when she was handed to me. I couldn't stop looking at her. She was the most beautiful infant, with a round, cherubic face, and she had a mischievous glint in her eyes. I knew from day one that she was going to be a mix of magic and trouble.

She could talk before she could walk. Nothing was sacred. When she was three, we'd get the bus into town every week. The same man used to get on, a very well-dressed guy carrying a briefcase. He was a little person, about the same height as Triona.

I'd give Triona a look that said, 'Don't open your mouth,' but every time she saw him she'd ask at the top of her voice, 'Why is that man so small?'

The poor man would get angry and I'd get a belt of his briefcase on my leg as he got off the bus. At home I'd sit Triona down and explain that there were all different kinds of people in the world and that it wasn't nice to talk about them out loud. The following week, she'd do the exact same thing, as if she wanted to get me into trouble.

The day she turned four, I dragged her into school, because it was either that or the social worker would have been called to take her away. I was barely coping.

When I collected her from school, the teacher would say, 'She won't sit down for us, she won't stop talking, there's no authority she'll listen to.' I had no answers, so I started sending Frances to collect her rather than face the barrage of complaints.

At the same time, things had settled down between Anthony and me. We'd gotten used to each other, and to the life we had together. We'd grown up, I suppose. We'd left the flat in Blackrock just before I got pregnant with Triona and moved into social housing, the Mayfield estate on the northside of Cork. Frances, her husband, Joe, and two children lived just a street away and our two families became joined at the hip.

For all of Triona's wildness, we really wanted another child. We tried and tried, but nothing was happening. Meanwhile Frances's husband would only have to put his pants on the end of the bed and she'd be pregnant. Month after month I would complain to her when my period came, and as time went on both myself and Anthony began to think we'd never have another baby.

Then, in 1989, six years after Triona came along, I became pregnant with Leanne. We were both over the moon with the news. Things were good financially, Triona had settled down a lot, and we had a good life. It seemed like the perfect time for our family to grow.

Frances fell pregnant again at the exact same time, with twins, so we were expecting together. Because of my experience going so overdue with Triona, I went private with a man called Dr Mondo. I told him my baby was due on 10 March and that I wanted her born on 10 March. I didn't want to go a minute past midnight.

When I had my first scan, we found that I was four months gone, rather than three months. I was delighted, because for me the nine months of pregnancy have always been more of an ordeal than the birth itself. Those forty weeks, which is closer to ten months when you think about it, seem to go on for ever.

I had trouble walking as time went on. Dr Mondo said that Leanne was leaning on a nerve, so I had to 'feather my nest'. Those were his exact words.

'What did he mean by that?' asked Frances.

'From now on I have to keep my legs up,' I replied.

'For God's sake!' said Frances. 'How am I going to get around?'

This was because I was the designated driver. I took our two families everywhere in the white van Anthony and I owned.

For the rest of the pregnancy, I did very little. Anthony would come home from work to make my lunch; he'd cook the dinner in the evenings. Frances looked after my kids, along with her own, and we muddled along very well. Even though I was severely restricted, I was delighted with life.

I got all these beautiful baby clothes knitted by a neighbour in Mayfield. They were so tiny they looked as if they'd fit a Barbie doll. When Leanne was born, she was nine pounds and hardly Barbie proportions!

I bounced through the doors of the hospital on Sunday, 9 March, as if I was going on a holiday rather than to give birth. Most people hate going into hospitals, but I was beyond excited. I wanted this baby so much!

Dr Mondo broke my waters at 8 p.m. and Leanne was born at 8 a.m. the following morning. Anthony was the first person to hold her. That was when the bond between them formed, I think. He's very close to Anthony and Triona, too, but I think there was a special connection between him and Leanne.

He held her for so long, I had to ask him to pass her down to me.

She was a quiet little thing, the spitting image of Triona as a newborn, only longer. She was real pretty, and you'd know straight away that she was a girl. She cuddled in to me immediately, and I felt so much love, it was like I wanted to eat her. I think I'd already bonded with her because I had been so looking forward to meeting her. We'd waited so long to get pregnant.

I felt complete. I wanted to be left alone to go over every little detail of her. Triona had picked out her name, and when I saw her I thought she did look like a Leanne.

She was mine. I didn't even want to give a bit of her to Anthony. I'd hoped for six children when I got married, but I knew when Leanne was born that she would be my last. That moment, when she cuddled into me, it was almost as if I knew the bones of her. I was literally flooded with love and happiness.

Little did I know she was going to cause me so much heartbreak.

8

I ended up staying in hospital for seven days after Leanne was born. My blood pressure was a bit low, nothing more than that, but the doctor insisted on keeping me in.

I couldn't sleep on the ward, and I think that was when my anxiety about Leanne began. There had been a few cot deaths in Mayfield the previous year, and I started thinking about them as I lay awake at night, the ward lit only by the eerie glow of the emergency exit signs.

One night I found myself whipped up into a frenzy of worry about Leanne. All the clothes I had for her were too big, and I thought she'd catch her death of cold in them. I called Frances in a state, telling her I needed her to get me a tiny woollen hat. I was sure that all the heat in Leanne's body was escaping through her head.

Poor Frances was only two weeks off having twins and I had her out searching the shops for a little knitted hat the next day.

Given that I lost Leanne eighteen years later, almost to the day of her birth, isn't it strange that, at the beginning of her life, I was terrified that she was going to die? Looking back on it, maybe I had post-natal depression, but at the time all I could think about was warding off her death. I was like some wild-eyed bodyguard, on constant high alert.

Although I'd bottle-fed Ant and Triona, before Leanne was born I was intent on breastfeeding her. But on the first day of her life, I decided against it. I witnessed a woman on the ward having great difficulty feeding her newborn. For hours she struggled in agony, trying to latch the baby on. After that I felt too anxious to try.

Along with my anxiety that Leanne was going to die, my old feelings of self-loathing were beginning to surface. I'd used the focus on my marriage and the first two children to keep those ugly feelings at bay, pushing the memories of my abuse firmly out of my mind, but for some reason the joy of having Leanne, after wanting her for so long, made them come back. Part of me thought I didn't deserve joy.

The day before I left the hospital, I asked my mam, Frances and Rosarie to clean my house from top to bottom. They were all women who made cleaning look like a magic trick – they'd have a home sparkling and you wouldn't have seen it being done – but when I got home, I felt it wasn't clean enough. I had them wiping the walls down with Milton to get rid of the germs I was sure the house was teeming with.

My sister gave me a second-hand sterilising unit for the bottles, but I couldn't bear to use it. I was afraid that Leanne would get an infection, so I had to have a new one.

If I changed Leanne and she didn't have a dirty nappy, I'd be crying, 'Oh, my God! She's constipated!' If she'd dirtied her nappy, I'd be crying, 'Oh, my God, she's gastric!'

In this constant state of anxiety, the worst of it all was that I still couldn't sleep. I was afraid that, if I so much as closed my eyes, Leanne was going to be taken.

Frances was the only one who could talk to me. 'You're having a meltdown,' she told me one day. 'You need to get some sleep or you won't be able to go on.'

I wouldn't go up to my bedroom, so Frances brought me into the sitting room and told me to lie down on the couch. She settled Leanne in her Moses basket beside me, put a blanket over me and tucked me in.

I wonder what Frances must have thought as I tried to nod off. She's not here now to tell me, God rest her soul, but she must have been extremely worried about me. I wasn't normally a high-anxiety kind of person. In many ways I'd become like her older sister, the solid unflappable one who took care of everyone. Maybe she was thinking of what I'd talked to her about not so long previously, the story of the little white mouse and how my childhood ended.

She sat with me for a bit, as a mother would with her child at bedtime, and for a moment I was able to let go, to allow myself drift away.

I was ten days home when Frances went into labour. Word came down from her house that she needed me. I knew she would take help from nobody but me, but I didn't know how I was going to leave Leanne. Anthony was at work, and although he'd gotten the news about Frances, it would be a while before he could get home.

I phoned my neighbour, Sheila. She'd spent a lot of time with my other children, and she loved them. I was still worried about leaving Leanne with her, but I had to get to Frances.

I ran up to Frances's house and found her in her bedroom, yelling. She was so big with the twins, she couldn't get down the stairs.

'My waters have broken, Collette,' she cried. 'Jesus, I'm in terrible pain!'

I could see her husband Joe was trying to stay cool and I tried to do likewise. But at the same time I was thinking, *These two babies are going to be born in this room and I haven't the first clue what to do.*

So I took a breath and asked my sister, 'Where's the bag you packed for the hospital?'

Frances pointed at two suitcases. I picked them up and flung them down the stairs, one after the other, shouting at Joe to phone a taxi.

I managed to get Frances to the top of the stairs, and then her second waters went. By the time the taxi arrived, she was in full labour.

I got in the back of the car with Frances, Joe got in the front, and together we encouraged her to keep panting instead of pushing. Leonard the taxi driver put his pedal to the metal and off we went speeding through the streets of Cork.

By the time we got to the hospital, Frances was already giving birth to the first of the twins. She was born on a stretcher, little Leazelle. The second, a boy, came seven minutes later, a breech birth. Frances named him Leonard, after the taxi driver, because only for him she never would have gotten to the hospital for such a difficult delivery.

When everything was over, my only thought was of getting back to Leanne. But something about the drama I'd gone through with Frances helped ease my anxiety. Maybe that intense experience, and the joy of seeing my beautiful new niece and nephew come into the world, punctured my post-natal depression. My fears about Leanne dying began to fade, and I was able to start appreciating that my baby girl was alive and well and thriving.

9

From the moment she was born, Leanne was a daddy's girl. Even as a very small child, she would play us against each other. If she asked me for something and I said, 'No,' she would ask her dad, and he'd say, 'Yes.' After a while we realised that we had to stick together. Otherwise Leanne was going to walk all over us.

If we said, 'No,' Leanne would start up with 'Please, can I? Please, can I?' Three weeks later she'd still be wearing us down.

Truth be told, we spoiled her rotten. It's something in the darkest days that I looked back on and wondered about. If we'd been as strict with Leanne as we were with Ant and Triona, would she have ended up so vulnerable? It was very difficult to say no to her, hard not to want to fulfil her every wish. She had that kind of effect on everyone.

She wasn't greedy, though. You might get her a new toy, and a day or two later, it would be nowhere to be found. She'd have given it away to some other child on the estate. They would ask could they play with it and she'd give it to them for keeps. She had a very generous heart, like that. She loved sharing.

She had a way of working things to her advantage. When she was ten we went to Tenerife on holidays and visited a sea park. In one of the shows, people were picked from the audience to swim with dolphins. Leanne, who loved animals, was enchanted.

She insisted on going back to the sea park again the next day, and when we went to see the dolphin show, she guided us to where she wanted to sit.

'She's a smart one.' Triona laughed. 'Wait till you see.'

Leanne knew exactly what she was doing. She'd sat exactly where they'd pick her to swim with the dolphins. We got such lovely photographs of her that day, having the time of her life with those dolphins surrounding her. Looking at them is still hard to bear.

Leanne was the ultimate people person. Wherever we went, she would always ask if someone else could come with us. We'd go on family holidays and she'd meet other children who would tag along for the whole time. If she went up to Frances's house to have her dinner, she'd meet someone along the way, and they'd come with her to eat. And it wouldn't just be other children – it didn't matter what age they were: from one to twenty, Leanne would bring them with her. She loved school, not because of the learning but because of her teachers and the kids in her class. She wanted their company.

After she died and I read in her diaries what had been happening, the bullying and ostracisation, my heart was torn in two for her. Anyone would hate to be isolated, but Leanne, who got her life energy from being with other people, must have felt it like a physical pain.

My favourite thing about Leanne was how she could make me laugh. No matter what trouble I was in, she could have me weeping with laughter. That's why I called her the light of my life. She made everything seem easier.

Given the heartbreak she caused me, it's strange now to look back on myself, bent in two, laughing uproariously as she egged me on. It gives me some comfort to remember her so joyful, but it's hard, too, because her death wiped out all the laughter. For a long time after she went, I thought I'd never laugh again.

Leanne was the typical youngest child, adored by everybody. She'd have fights with Triona, the way sisters often do, over clothes or make-up or what-have-you, but the two of them were very tight. Her brother was like another father to her. He loved the bones of her, and she had him wrapped around her little finger, always getting him to give her money so she could buy things for herself.

Ant and Triona have both lived with their own terrible pain and guilt since she died. No one thinks about the siblings of a suicide victim, how it impacts on them. In recent years, I've met many brothers and sisters who have lost siblings to suicide, and I can tell you it shatters their lives.

My desperate fear of Leanne dying might have waned within a few months of her birth, but that didn't mean we didn't have to be on high alert. Leanne had a few close shaves in her childhood.

Anthony and I were in the front room one night, watching television, and Leanne and Triona were playing in the kitchen. Leanne was about five at the time and, unbeknownst to me, the two of them were fooling around with the kettle, pressing its button on and off.

I called into them that it was Leanne's bedtime, but I could hear her giggles getting louder and louder. Her laughter was infectious and I started giggling, too. Then I heard her scream.

The kettle had fallen off the counter and its boiling contents had spilled all over Leanne. Pandemonium broke out, Anthony dialling 999 while I tried to rip Leanne's clothes off. I was beside myself with panic, but Triona was very quick-thinking. She said we couldn't wait for the ambulance: we'd have to run cold water over Leanne. The poor child looked like she was going into shock – the boiling water had poured down all over her face and neck and chest.

We took her up to the bathroom, ran her under cold water and then wrapped her in a quilt. The ambulance hadn't arrived yet, so we got into the car with her to drive to the hospital. Leanne was hysterical. 'Mammy, Mammy, it's burning!' she cried, as I held her on the back seat. What I didn't realise was that the skin continues to burn. They explained it to us in the hospital afterwards.

They were worried that she might lose her left eye, but luckily a specialist was able to save it. She suffered third-degree burns, though. She lost all the freckles on one side of her face, and for the rest of her life you could see where the water had scalded her. She lost so many layers of skin that moisturisers and sunscreen actually burned her if she put them on. I had fierce trouble in the sun with her if we went on holidays.

A couple of months later she became very ill with pneumonia. I always felt it was related to the scalding, because after she got out of hospital I knew something wasn't right. I brought her to the doctor about four times in two weeks, but he couldn't pinpoint anything wrong. He must have thought I was being a paranoid mother.

She stopped eating and drinking to the point that I had to feed her teaspoons of tea, to get some liquid into her. In the end, I went to the doctor and stood my ground. 'There's something really wrong with her,' I insisted.

He sent her for X-rays and when I looked at them, her lungs were completely clouded over. She had double pneumonia, we were told. She was so sick that worries she might die began haunting me again.

I often think those anxieties were a kind of premonition. She was only five years old at the time, but when you think about it, Leanne didn't have very long left to live.

10

My auntie Frances was my favourite person in the whole world. She was like my second mother. Frances died five years ago. At first I couldn't talk about her, never mind mention her name, but now as time has passed I've learned that talking about her makes me feel better.

**From 'A Bit About Me' by Leanne Wolfe –
transition year school project**

Frances died on Leanne's eleventh birthday. Later, when I came to read Leanne's diaries, I would see what she had written about it.

How could anybody forget somebody as wonderful as Frances?

It hurt to read those words, because they felt like a reproach. When we went to the hospital that day, Frances had already passed away and Leanne was inconsolable. 'You'll never forget her,' I said, in an effort to comfort her.

I think now about the effect Frances's illness and death had on Leanne, how the grief might have weakened her and made her open to the darkness we learned about in her diaries. Leanne adored Frances. All through her childhood, she followed my sister around like she was her shadow.

In 1997 they found a tumour on the back wall of Frances's chest, and when they went in to remove it, they discovered it was attached to her heart and lungs. She had open-heart surgery and her lungs had to be deflated, but they couldn't remove the tumour. This was the start of Frances's long journey with cancer.

Looking back, I think maybe her journey began when she lost little Leazelle, who died from meningitis at the age of one. Frances never fully recovered from the tragedy. It was like a little light went out in her eyes and didn't come back on. She got through, she learned to laugh again, and she had three more children, but the grief was always just beneath the surface. Maybe it turned to sickness.

The three years of Frances's illness were very hard on our two families. The rounds of chemotherapy and radiation, the sickness, the bad turns, the tiredness, the surgeries, the disappointments, the terror. The cancer couldn't be kept at bay. Frances was a very strong woman, but by the end the cancer was everywhere. It was actually coming out through her skin, a horrible kind of discolouring.

I remember her asking me, 'Collette, what's that?'

'It's just pigmentation,' I told her.

The children were at the mercy of the cancer, too. No plans could be made and kept because there was always another crisis on the horizon. The sickness hung over their lives, the terrible fear that their mother, their auntie, was not going to survive.

My beloved sister, whom I'd relied on since I was a child, like she was my own mother, and who had come to rely on me in the same way, was dying before my very eyes, and I couldn't accept it. We were seen by everyone in Mayfield as the one family. I felt her children were like my children; she felt the same about my own. She was good for the cleaning and I'd do the cooking. I drove us everywhere and she did the shopping. We were a great team.

Before she passed, she recorded messages for each of her children on cassette tapes, and for each of mine.

When she asked if I wanted her to record one for me, I said no. If I'd said yes, it would have been admitting that she was going to leave me, and I wasn't prepared to do that.

I don't know if it's a tradition anywhere else in the world, but on St Stephen's Day the men in Cork go out to get their two free Christmas pints in their local pub. On Frances's last Stephen's Day, Anthony was getting ready to go out. He said he'd take the children, to give Frances and myself a break, but as he was all about to go out the door, he stopped.

'I'm not going,' he said. 'I think there's no better place in the world than right here today.'

If you could have seen the smile that lit up Frances's face. She whispered to me, 'Anthony is a good man.'

I whispered back, 'He loves you, Frances. We all do.'

I looked at my husband as he took his coat off, and thought about the kindness of his nature. Over the last three years I'd watched him with Frances's children and with our own, how he was so gentle with them, so attentive. He took such great care of Frances, too – always ready to help her at the drop of a hat, always quietly there for her.

Some people wait a long time for their eyes to open. I'd always been respectful towards Anthony, had always made an effort in our marriage – we had a date night every week, even when we didn't have two cents to rub together. He had become my best friend, but there had always been a part of me held away from him because I was still afraid of men. I still feared getting hurt.

The compassion he had for Frances was spread before me and I realised this man could never hurt me. This man had been doing the opposite of hurting me from the moment I'd met him. He had been loving me. My heart opened to him that day. In the midst of losing Frances, my eyes were opened to love.

She died less than three months later. We'd been planning a big party in the Mardyke for Leanne's birthday – Frances had insisted on it.

'She's missed out on a lot, with everything going on,' Frances said. She'd given Leanne her present already, a beautiful morning coat.

Frances was all excited about the party, too, but two nights before it was to take place, she had a bad turn and went into the hospital. In a couple of days, things went from bad to worse, so by the morning of Leanne's birthday, I'd forgotten all about it. I'd stayed with Frances in her hospital room the previous night. She was still conscious, still talking, so I thought this was just another turn, that she'd be home again.

I left the hospital at seven that morning. Frances didn't want me to go, but I was exhausted.

'I'm falling down with the tiredness,' I told her. 'I'm literally shattered by you, girl.' We laughed at that.

When I got home, Anthony opened the door and said, 'You need to go back to the hospital.'

When I got back, Frances was in the bed, looking like a tiny, frightened rabbit. She'd brought up a teaspoon of blood and she was so freaked out, she'd told the nurse to call for me.

'Mother of God, girl, you didn't spit up a lung!' I reassured her. 'It's just a little bit of blood.'

But my heart was racing because I knew her time was near.

I had to get some sleep, so I left her again. She died a few hours later.

I remember looking at Leanne when we got to the hospital to say our final goodbyes, and it dawned on me that it was her birthday. I tried to comfort her, but I was in shock myself. Even though Frances was so sick, there was a part of me that thought she wouldn't die, that it wasn't possible.

The party didn't happen, of course, and Leanne never said a word of complaint, but in her diary she begged the question: 'Why did Frances have to die on my birthday?'

When my daughter was found dead in her room seven years later, she had the morning coat she'd gotten from Frances wrapped around her. On the phone from Lanzarote I asked the paramedics to cover her with it, rather than with a sheet, as they took her body from our house.

11

You could write a whole book about the night my father died. It was two days before Christmas and he was seventy-two. He'd been acting up for weeks, giving my mam a tough time with the drink. He'd fall up Tory Top Road every night after closing time, and it's a hill. Sometimes he'd have to be carried up.

A couple of nights before he died my mam was very upset. 'I have to drag him to the house no matter where he falls,' she told me. 'I'm not able to do it any more.'

'Leave him where he falls,' I said. 'Throw a blanket over him and leave him there.'

The night he died, Dunnes Stores was open for

twenty-four hours for the first time ever, because of the Christmas trade. Frances wasn't feeling well, so I said to her, 'I'll go to Dunnes and get your shopping.' I was worried about her. Leanne, who was eight at the time, had a bout of the flu that was going around, but Frances seemed sick in a different way. She'd lost weight and there were dark circles under her eyes.

When I got to the supermarket at around 11 p.m., there were queues a mile long behind every till. People had gone mad for the all-night shopping. After a long wait, I was near the top of a queue when I looked behind me and saw my mam with my sister, Rosarie, at the very back. Mam looked so tired. She couldn't take another step.

I said to the girl on the till, 'Can I bring my mam up to the top of the queue?' and she said I could. When we got all the shopping paid for and packed, I told Rosarie that I'd bring Mam home in my car.

When we got to her house, we pulled up outside and my mam went in ahead of me. I was carrying the shopping through the gate, when I saw Mam running past the hall and into the front room that she always used to keep locked. It was her domain, that room, a place where she could have some time to herself. Nobody was allowed inside.

Then Rosarie ran out, shouting, 'My dad is dead!'

I threw my eyes up to Heaven. 'Sure he's been dying for twenty years,' I said, and it was true. He'd pretended a load of times that he'd had a heart attack, stretching himself out on the floor as if he was about to take his last breath. An ambulance would be called and by the time they got him to the hospital, he'd get back up off the gurney and he'd be grand. All the tests said his heart was fine.

'No, Collette, he's really dead this time,' my sister said. 'He's in the kitchen.'

He must have been leaning against a cupboard and had slipped down to the floor. My first feeling was relief. He had caused my mother so much trouble in life, his death might unburden her.

My relief was short-lived. We called for an ambulance, and when it arrived, the paramedics said, 'You're going to have to get the guards.'

'Why?' I asked.

Rosarie had told them she and my mam had left the house at 10 p.m. It was around midnight when we found him, but the paramedics said the timing wasn't possible. He was dead a lot longer than three hours.

I thought back to what I'd told my mother: *Leave him where he falls*. She'd been cooking a ham for the Christmas dinner earlier. Had he just fallen down in the kitchen while she was doing it and she'd left him there?

I asked Rosarie, 'Was Dad in the house when you collected Mam for the supermarket?'

She said he wasn't, so I went and knocked on the

door of the front room, where my mam was locked inside. 'Was my dad here when you went to the supermarket?' I asked her.

'He wasn't,' she cried, through the door. 'He wasn't here at all!'

The guards arrived. Half of Tory Top Road was outside the house at that stage, including my dad's alcoholic friends.

One of the guards was talking to the paramedics. I asked them if they'd need my dad's medical history from his GP, saying I could phone for it tomorrow.

'I was in this house before,' the guard said.

In the early eighties my brother kept a horse at the side of our house. We had a big corner garden, so it grazed there. One of my dad's drunken buddies had phoned the garda station and said, 'Shergar is at fifty-four Tory Top Road.'

Shergar was this massively expensive racehorse that had disappeared from a stud in Kildare. All the newspapers were writing about him at the time.

The guards took the call seriously and they descended on our house. They came from everywhere, surrounding the place, but they soon figured that the nag in our garden was no million-dollar thoroughbred.

'We still laugh inside the station about it,' the guard told me, as my father lay dead on our kitchen floor.

'It wasn't very funny for us at the time,' I said.

The parish priest arrived and started commiserating

with my dad's drinking buddies. 'He was a lovely man,' he said, and they all nodded, like wise old men. 'He used to come to mass every morning.'

I wanted to say, 'You haven't a clue, Father. He was a street angel and a house devil,' but I kept my lip buttoned.

In the meantime, the undertakers had arrived, but they had to wait for my father's GP to come before they could take him.

We were all sitting around the table, myself, my sisters, the guards, the priest and the undertaker, when Dr Ryan arrived. He took one look at my father, then went out and knocked on the door of the front room. 'Annie, can I come in?' he said.

My mam unlocked the door and let him in. He stayed in there with her for half an hour while we waited in the kitchen with Dad's body. When he came out, the doctor explained to everyone that my dad had had hardened arteries and that was the reason rigor mortis had set in so quickly.

Charlie Sullivan was the undertaker. He was by himself, so he asked me if I'd help carry the body.

'Ah, for God's sake, Charlie, there's no way we're helping you take my dad out our front door,' I said.

It was coming up to six o'clock in the morning and Charlie had to call for his lads to get out of their beds to help him.

When they were bringing him through the house,

they needed to back into the front room so they could get Dad's body outside. Mam refused to unlock the door. 'He was never allowed in here when he was alive,' she said. 'He's not coming in here dead!'

They had to reverse him up the stairs and back out the front.

We had terrible storms all over that Christmas, so none of my sisters and brothers living in England could get here. We postponed the funeral, but when eventually they were able to make it, the gravediggers went on strike. It took ten days before my dad was finally buried.

Every alcoholic in Ireland was at the funeral and they drank the bar dry at the lunch afterwards. I remember Mam putting a thousand pounds in my hand so I wouldn't have to shell out buying drinks. None of us drank a drop ourselves, because she wasn't drinking. We wanted to respect her.

It wasn't a sad funeral for me and I didn't really grieve for him. My dad had caused enough trouble while he was alive. Of course my life was changed with his passing, but not in a bad way. It wouldn't be long until another member of my family passed away, and this time it would be a terrible loss in my life.

12

When Leanne was in sixth class she was assessed and identified as dyslexic. I did everything in my power to get her the help she needed, to let every teacher know about it, and to try and make sure her self-confidence didn't suffer because of it. But I didn't make any link between her dyslexia and the fact that I couldn't read or write myself.

When I was growing up I didn't understand why my sisters could read and I couldn't. I would often hold a pencil in my hand and pretend to be writing, but I wouldn't be able to put anything down because I couldn't spell. It took me a long time to learn to spell my own name.

At school, nobody asked, 'Do you need help with that?' Somebody must have noticed, but probably they thought I was slow, that I wasn't worth bothering with.

After leaving school, I avoided anything to do with writing like the plague. I always had an excuse, a way to get out of a sticky situation. I was a great bluffer – for years even my children didn't know I couldn't read or write. And beneath it all, my inability to put words together on a page only added to the shame I felt.

After I left Byrne's meat-processing factory, I worked for years as a cleaner. I didn't need writing skills to do it and I would leave a place immaculate, taking pride in that. I always got more jobs because I was so good at it.

Anthony had his work cut out trying to persuade me to go with him to the bank for our first mortgage. I'll never forget the humiliation I felt that day. I could only print my name on the forms. Everything else had to be filled in on my behalf. I wanted to crawl away into a corner. I could imagine the bank manager thinking, *Look at this grown woman with her own children and she can't even fill in a form*. It nearly pushed me over the edge.

Years later, after I'd let Anthony in on the truth, he tried to teach me to read. He wasn't a natural teacher, and I wasn't what you might call a relaxed student. We nearly killed each other.

Frances tried to teach me, too, but no matter how I tried to follow her instruction, the words came out wrong. I didn't find out that I was dyslexic until after she died.

In an effort to get me back on my feet again, Triona and Ant signed me up for a FÁS computer course, without telling me. I was very reluctant when I found out but, because they'd gone to a lot of bother, I decided to give it a shot.

The course was a turning point for me. I wasn't looked down upon or made to feel stupid. I learned how to use computers and that opened a new world for me. There was work experience to be done as part of the course, but it was all office work. The course leader suggested that I sign up for an adult literacy course.

A few weeks into that, the teacher took me aside and told me, 'Collette, you are profoundly dyslexic.'

I was thrilled with the news! Don't get me wrong, I didn't want to be dyslexic, but having it identified put a lot of things into perspective for me. It was proof I wasn't as stupid as I'd thought I was.

I've often said to Anthony that MI5 should actually recruit dyslexics. Words, letters and numbers may get mixed up in my head, but I have an almost photographic memory for other things. I can recall an entire conversation that happened years ago – I never forget a name or a person's story.

At the end of the FÁS course, the work-experience placements were coming up, but because I wouldn't be able to work in an office, I hadn't a clue what to go for. My dream job, and you may laugh to read this, was with Marks & Spencer. When the children were young, I'd bring them in there, and the shop assistants were always kind to me. They had a class about them, a sense of confidence in what they were doing. I'd think about what it would be like to work there, to be one of those people. But I was a cleaner who couldn't even read or write, so I figured the likes of Marks & Spencer was completely out of my reach.

When the FÁS course leader asked me what I might like to do for work experience, I blurted out, 'I'd love to go to Marks & Spencer's.'

'Oh, Collette, I'm sorry,' she said. 'We don't do placements there. But you could approach them yourself, if you like.'

I gave that suggestion a big fat no, but after a few days I decided there was no harm in asking. Sure what was the worst they could say?

So I approached M&S. Actually, I phoned them about a hundred times. And then my niece Jessica phoned them, and then the FÁS course leader phoned them. Eventually the HR manager, a woman called Mary McCrumm, said to me, 'Come in for a chat.'

I cannot tell you how huge this was for me. To

be working in a nice place like that, where I wasn't hidden, where I'd get to meet people, all kinds of people! The first thing Mary McCrumm said to me when I went to meet her was 'What's your name again?'

I was so overwhelmed I couldn't remember my own name! I had to stand there, trying to get myself together, while she stared at me in silence. But, still, once I settled down and started talking, Mary told me they were going to give me a month's work experience.

I'd say I was one of the hardest workers they ever got. I'd be in there before my starting time and I always finished late. I did things I wasn't supposed to do, mucked in and helped in whatever way I could, all the time not stepping on any toes, making sure I was as respectful as possible. And I loved every minute of it. Some people say a religious life is their calling, some say being a teacher is theirs, but I can honestly say working at M&S was mine.

Word got around that I'd be an asset to the company and I was told I'd be given an interview for a permanent position. It would be in three stages. The first two were a phone interview with someone at head office, and a practical, where I'd be secretly watched on the floor, seeing how I handled the customers. The third stage involved written answers.

I hadn't told Mary I was dyslexic, because I'd thought it would go against me, and now I didn't want to say anything because it might jeopardise my chances. The written part of the interview took place on a Friday, the very last day of my work experience. I remember thinking, *They're going to let me go after this and I won't ever come back into this shop again.*

It was one of my busiest days there so far – the place was jammed – but a couple of hours before I was supposed to finish, someone came by my station and said, 'Collette, they're looking for you up in HR.'

The woman in HR was called Rose. She said, 'It's manic today, but I've been told to give you your interview anyway. You wouldn't mind telling me your answers to the questions and I'll type them in? It will hurry things up.'

What were the odds on that? 'No problem,' I replied, relief flooding through me.

They told me that day that I had the job and I skipped out of the place, high on life. It was the first feeling of lightness I'd had since Frances had left me.

I didn't tell anyone in M&S for years that I'm dyslexic. Because I hadn't mentioned it at the outset, I felt it was better to say nothing at all. I'd learned to bluff it anyway, when I'd thought my inability to read and write was just a matter of my stupidity. I managed to work it at M&S so that I'd never have to fill out a form of any kind.

To begin with, Leanne's journey with dyslexia was less

complicated. She didn't have to study Irish in secondary school and she was given special dispensations in the Junior Cert. But sadly her dyslexia would play a part in the downward spiral that led to her suicide.

13

About a year before Frances died, we moved to Rathcormac, which was about a half-hour drive from Cork City. I'd needed to get out of Mayfield, because although I couldn't accept that Frances might leave us, I knew things were going to change big-time.

When we first took Frances to see the house, she wept because it was so far away. 'I can see the Dublin lights,' she cried.

After Frances was gone, I could hardly bear to go back to Mayfield, but Leanne, who was especially close to Frances's son, Leonard, kept a close connection with the place. It would turn out to be the undoing of her.

Apart from moving away from Mayfield because of Frances, I felt there was a better place for me to raise my children. It wasn't snobbery: it was just that kids could get into a lot of trouble with drink and drugs in Mayfield. When we were living there we had to do a lot of work with Ant and Triona to keep them focused, to put college into their heads and steer a safe path for them.

I think football saved my son from going down the road so many boys his age did. He was dedicated to staying healthy – Ant's body is his temple. Triona wasn't a great mixer and she only had a couple of friends. Frances believed in limiting the children to two friends each so they wouldn't get into trouble. It was when they started hanging out in big gangs that things went astray.

Away from Mayfield and without Frances to keep an eye on Leanne, we forgot this philosophy.

Hindsight is a wonderful thing. You see the patterns. You see what you could have done, or not done, to change history. When you lose a child to suicide, you go over the past again and again with a fine-tooth comb, trying to figure out where you went wrong, to find ways to pin the blame on yourself. The guilt is overwhelming.

After Frances's death I wasn't eating, I wasn't sleeping. I found it hard to get out the door. I would go to the phone, thinking, *I'll ring Frances*, and I'd have the phone in my hand before remembering that she was gone. I was so grief-stricken, I had to go on medication. Maybe I took my eye off the ball. Maybe I was so absorbed in my own feelings that I didn't pay attention to Leanne the way I had with her brother and sister.

Having said that, I always thought Leanne had a kind of emotional sense about her, that she could take care of herself better than the others. When I read her diaries, I found that she couldn't take care of herself at all.

The first inkling we had of trouble was when we discovered Leanne in 'the field'.

Mayfield was surrounded by farmers' fields and gangs of teenagers would hang out in them, getting up to no good with booze and drugs. The field was off limits for Ant and Triona. We told them there would be serious consequences if they were so much as glimpsed there.

One day, when Leanne was fourteen, Anthony and I drove up to Mayfield to collect her from Frances's house, but there was no sign of her. I asked one of the children where she was and I was told she'd gone to the field. Anthony and I jumped into the car and went speeding off to find her. We got out and stood at the top of the hill, where we could see Leanne with a small group of boys and girls.

Anthony was livid. 'Leanne!' he roared. 'Get your ass up here, right now!'

She strolled up as slow as you like, a proper expression of teenage aggravation on her face. All the way home, she kept up her complaints. 'I wasn't doing anything wrong! You mortified me!'

'We didn't rear you to be in a field!' Anthony shouted at her. 'You're not going there again, do you hear me?'

When we got her home, she went straight up to her bedroom, locked her door and put on loud music, which we could hear pounding through the ceiling.

In her diary that day, she wrote about Anthony and me: 'I'll fix them. I'll wreck their heads.'

Reading those words, you'd think she was tough as nails, but the truth is that she was the opposite, too soft for her own good. One of the great regrets that surfaced in the early days after her death was that I hadn't toughened her up. Because I hated confrontation, I think I instilled the same sense of avoidance at all costs in my children, and especially in Leanne.

I felt I'd let her down as a mother. If I hadn't mollycoddled her, if I'd taught her to be more resilient, maybe she might have weathered the storm that was about to rage into her life.

14

My sister Annabelle was fifty when she died in 2003 of angina to the stomach. Maurice Gibb from the Bee Gees died of the same thing that year. It's a very curable disease, but it's not easy to detect, so Annabelle was well down the line with it before it became apparent to the doctors. She died only two weeks after the diagnosis and it was a horrendous death. She underwent a fifteen-hour operation, and when she came out they hadn't even been able to sew her back together.

My husband used to call her Pocahontas, she was so dark and naturally beautiful, but it was hard to recognise her when she died. She'd lost so much weight, and seeing her body was like looking at someone who had been underneath ice for a thousand years.

Annabelle lived in England and her wish was that she'd be cremated. My mam had never known anybody that was cremated, never even been to a funeral where the person wasn't buried. When we went to the cremation, it was like watching a conveyor belt. I'd never seen anything like it.

Mam was in a state of shock. She was handed an urn afterwards and she couldn't get her head around it. 'Is all of Annabelle in there?' she asked.

When we got home, I knew my mam was plotting something because she was on to Charlie Sullivan, the undertaker. She arranged a 'proper' funeral for Annabelle. She got a coffin made to put the urn into, and it was buried in the same graveyard as my dad, St Finbarr's cemetery. There were bagpipes in the church for her, and a service with a priest. So my sister was actually cremated *and* buried.

It could only have happened with my mam.

She took Annabelle's passing in the same quiet and dignified way she'd taken Frances's death. I remember thinking at the time, God almighty, why isn't she tearing her hair out? She's lost two daughters within three years.

To be truthful, I thought maybe there was a bit of coldness. She didn't express anything.

One night I was staying in her house when I heard her crying in her bedroom. I went in to comfort her. 'Why do you keep it all to yourself?' I asked her.

'I don't want to upset you or your sisters,' she said.

She would have the same forbearing reaction to Leanne's death, but it would take something away from her that neither Frances nor Annabelle's passing could. Both my sisters died of natural causes, and neither of them wanted to go. I could see in her eyes that, like all of our family, she couldn't come to terms with her beloved Leanne choosing to take her own life.

Sometimes people can become statistics, a number among the numbers who have died. With this book I want to show Leanne as more than a teenager who committed suicide. I want to show her humanity and, in doing so, show the humanity of all people who are brought to a point in life where they feel they can't go on.

I only have to look at a photograph of her and it brings back everything she was – a bright, funny, cheeky, lovable girl, who could wrap you around her little finger at the same time as giving you the shirt off her back. All parents say it about their own children, but there was something special about Leanne, something people were drawn to. It was a sparkling quality, an infectious sense of fun and mischievousness mixed with gentle kindness, the latter of which came from her father.

But she was a complicated girl, too, and highly sensitive, a lot more so than she let on. As a teen I developed a loud, devil-may-care front to mask the terrible vulnerability I felt inside. Leanne was fronting, too, in ways I did sense, and there were moments when she let the mask slip. Yet at the same time I was so caught up in the push and pull of our relationship that I didn't comprehend something deeper was going on.

In retrospect I see all the hints, and some major incidents stand out like the big red warning signs I should have paid serious heed to at the time. But back then I was the mother of a rebellious teenager with a will of iron. We clashed and the drama covered what was really going on. If I said, 'Black,' she would say, 'White,' and it was like she was angry with me all the time. I put it down to hormones flying all over the place. She'd ask me a question and I'd say, 'Leanne, whatever answer I give you, am I going to be safe?' Nothing I did or said seemed to be good enough for her.

Her trips to Mayfield continued, along with the calls I'd get to drive up there and collect her from Frances's house. One night when she got into the car, I thought I smelt booze off her.

'Leanne, have you been drinking?' I asked.

She was outraged. 'That's just lovely,' she said,

giving me a look that might have curdled milk. 'My own mother doesn't even trust me.'

It was a brand new car and, after a few minutes' driving in hostile silence, I realised the smell of alcohol I was getting came from the windscreen wash, the way it does on cars just out of the showroom.

I turned to Leanne and said, 'I'm sorry, girl. I made a mistake.'

She was so angry with me that she went off on a rant about what a terrible person I was, how I was always accusing her of things, how she'd be better off if she was drunk, how a mother like me would drive anyone to drink and drugs . . . On and on and on it went, until I could take no more.

We were near enough to Rathcormac, on a country road near a graveyard, when I snapped. 'Leanne,' I said, 'if you don't shut up, I'm stopping this car and you're getting out.'

'Stop the car!' she shouted.

We came to a halt and she flung the door open and stormed off into the darkness.

For a minute or two I waited for her to come back, but then I was so angry, I drove off. When I reached the house, I relented and turned round, but when I got to the graveyard, she was nowhere to be seen.

As I called out for her, a big truck came screeching past me. It had a kind of weird, lit-up skeleton sitting in the passenger seat, and a bolt of fear shot through me.

I thought the driver had taken her – that he'd thrown her into the back of his truck and was driving away with her. Of all people, I knew this world wasn't safe for young girls, and I'd left my own daughter stranded in the darkness on a deserted country road. I was so full of fear, I wanted to throw up.

I went racing back to the house and found Anthony. I didn't tell him exactly what had happened, but through my panic I tried to say I thought Leanne might have been kidnapped.

'She's upstairs in her room, Collette,' he said, giving me a strange look.

Leanne had hidden behind a hedge when she got out of the car, then walked home. She knew she was going to frighten the life out of me.

I must have been the colour of ash when I found her sitting up in her bed. The smirk of satisfaction on her face was second to none. She'd gotten her revenge.

We had this spitfire of a girl living with us, but outside the house she was beginning to get into real emotional trouble. It's not in the diaries, but piecing it together in the weeks and months after her death, I figured out how the bullying had begun.

Another girl was being picked on and Leanne stood up for her. She'd recently lost her father to cancer, this girl, and she was very vulnerable. I think the two ringleaders caught on to it and were making her life a misery. After we found Leanne's diaries, I talked to the girl and she told me that Leanne had intervened on her behalf.

The bullies couldn't have been very happy with that. For legal reasons I can't name them, so I'll call them Mary 1 and Mary 2. There's a picture I later found of them with Leanne at a teenage disco around this time, and you can see it in Leanne's face.

She's afraid.

15

Well, the past few days have certainly been the worst for me. Monday night I went to - - - - and we bumped into Mary 1 and she hit me straight into the face and I have a black eye. I am mortified. I couldn't even hit her back and now everyone is laughing at me.
This is going on too long, I can't go on with this shit no more, I can't live with it no more, I really can't. It's not fair. What did I ever

do to her or any of them for that matter?
If anything happens to me, I want this read
out in front of everyone at my funeral.

As any parent who has lost a child to suicide knows, the self-questioning never ends. Why was I not able to stop it? How did I not see it coming? And then there are the signs – which you didn't know were signs at the time, but which in hindsight are like sirens you can't believe you didn't hear.

Over and over it goes in your mind. If only I'd realised. If only she'd said something. If only I'd been shrewd enough to pick up on the truth. How I've castigated myself in the years since she died for not noticing, for not being a good enough mother that she'd come to me with her problems. How I've punished myself.

There were so many clues I might have picked up on. Leanne dressed for a teenage disco in a new outfit, complaining, 'Would you look at the size of me!' She was a normal size for her age, but out of the blue she suddenly thought she was obese. I thought it was just a thing that teenage girls go through, this obsession with weight, but later in her diaries I saw what was destroying her confidence. She was being constantly told she was fat.

Something else that became a regular occurrence,

but again I just put it down to teenage mood: Leanne coming home after being out with her friends, running straight up the stairs and shutting herself in her room. The loud music would go on – thump-thump-thump – and I'd think she was just trying to avoid having to be downstairs with her annoying mam and dad, or having to give us details about where she'd been.

Then there was the change in behaviour, more like a little girl, going back to wanting to be cuddled. I'd rejoice at these times because it was like having back the child I once knew. I didn't know that she was desperate for some comfort in her despair.

There were occasions when we saw what was going on, three in all, but they happened with such spaced-out timing, we thought they were isolated incidents.

The first was when she was fifteen and came home with a black eye. She was reluctant to tell Triona and me what happened, but eventually we got it out of her. She had been up in Mayfield and there was a big gang of them there, and Mary 1 started mocking her. Leanne answered her back and Mary 1 hit her in the face. She actually knocked Leanne to the ground. Leanne started crying and the gang of them – there must have been twelve teenagers – all started mocking her, throwing things at her.

Triona and I got into a car and drove around until we found Mary 1. I said if it happened again, I'd report her to the guards. Triona told her that if she ever laid a hand on Leanne again, that it wouldn't be the guards she'd be dealing with, it would be her. Our Triona, who was afraid of her own shadow!

We thought we had done the right thing, that we'd put a stop to it. We thought that was the end of the fighting. Her diaries told a different story. We had only made things worse.

You allowed smelly shithead dickface, L. touch you. Your ugly lookin size 14 pants are so tight on you I wouldn't be able to get them off your fattie chickpocked ass. Measlehead. With your polio fingernails and your ears worse than Dumbo! And your ass is so BIG it could form its own website. With your head so big I could fit ten of my heads into your one head. FATTIE!!! Whatca gona do bout it! You smelly fuckin pancake with your mushy earlobes. You smell like dog shit … I will get ur smelly pissy size 12 pants, rap them around ur fat smelly infested hickey neck and hang you out the window and leave the birds at you.

– a note handed to Leanne by one of her bullies

The bullying was constant and it went on for years. It leaked into every corner of Leanne's life and turned every good thing bad. Maybe she didn't tell us about it because she didn't want to bring it home. I've tried to comfort myself with that thought, the idea that we were a haven away from the suffering – that with her family was the one place where she could be safe.

But it doesn't work. I'm not comforted, because while we got on with our lives, while other events were happening in the family, like Triona's pregnancies and her marriage, or Ant moving in with his girlfriend, or me getting my job in Marks & Spencer, Leanne was up in her room, pouring her pain into a diary that she hid under her bed.

For a large part it's like any teenage girl's diary, with plenty of details about the boys she fancied, or the ones she 'met', which I discovered was teenage slang for 'kissed'. They're full of angst over fellas she thought she was in love with, or who she wished were in love with her. They're packed with the kind of intrigue that only goes on between teenage girls, the ups and downs of friendship, gossip about who 'met' who, and who's going to go crazy because their boyfriend was seen 'meeting' someone else.

They detail her first sexual experience, which was hard to read about, and a pregnancy scare exacerbated by a dream she had of Frances, who appeared in her bedroom to tell her she was going to have a baby.

They list more sex, and nights out drinking to the point of becoming paralytic, and plans for more nights out and more drinking and smoking joints. There are declarations like 'today and yesterday were the hardest days of my life!' after a break-up with a boyfriend we knew nothing about at the time.

There's love and betrayal and heartache and annoyance and complaints and happiness and sadness and excitement, the whole frenzy of that time in a girl's life when childhood is behind her and she's awake to the intrigues of the world.

But there are also statements like 'I'm going to get shit-kicked to death,' and 'All I'm thinking about is killing myself but the only thing what's stopping me is my mam and dad.'

There was so much going on in Leanne's life that we hadn't the first clue about, so many secrets. At times since she died, I've felt angry towards her for keeping those secrets. I've been overwhelmed by the extent of them. I've felt shame for wanting to read things in her diaries about me, pronouncements that she loved me, and that I was a good mother after all.

But there are no such pronouncements. Anthony, Triona, Ant and I hardly figure in those pages. Instead they are a window into a world away from us all and a life that was silently coming apart at the seams.

One of the most awful things to read about is her shame. Although I blamed her bullies for it, I also associated it with my own secret shame. Somehow I felt I'd passed it on to her.

16

When we told Leanne she would be getting a car for her seventeenth birthday, she was thrilled. We'd sold the house in Rathcormac because we wanted to be nearer the city, and we were downsizing, so we had a bit of extra cash. We'd decided on a small car, a Toyota Aygo, but when we took Leanne to the dealership, she said, 'I'm not driving that car.'

'Don't start, Leanne,' I said. 'It's either that or no car.'

'I'd be ashamed to be seen in that thing,' Leanne replied.

Anthony seemed to be in shock. He couldn't speak.

'Look what you're driving, Mam,' Leanne complained. 'And you want me to drive that shitty car?'

I had a new Avensis at the time. With the money coming in from my job at M&S, and Anthony's construction business, we were doing well. 'I work hard and I paid for my own car,' I told Leanne, but she wouldn't back down.

She spotted a Yaris in the corner of the showroom and said, 'I'll take one of those. In metallic black. I don't want the five-door because that's for families. I want a hatchback. And alloy wheels.'

The next thing I knew, we were ordering the Yaris. Leanne had that kind of effect on us. We couldn't say no.

On the way home from the showroom, she was hyper. 'I can't wait to get it!' she was saying. 'When will it be ready, Mam?'

Anthony fumed at the wheel.

'Mam!' Leanne said. 'When you collect the car will you fill it up with balloons before you bring it to me?'

'I'll give you balloons!' Anthony roared. He wanted to kill her!

'For God's sake, Leanne,' I said, turning around to her. 'Don't you ever know when to shut your mouth?'

But two weeks later, on our way to collect the car, we stopped at a shop to buy packets of balloons. We blew them up and filled the car with them for her, and from her reaction, it was worth it. She threw her arms around us both. She was ecstatic.

Reading her diaries from that time, I was glad we'd brought a moment of pure joy into her life, although I knew we were giving in to her too much.

There's no doubt that we spoiled Leanne – something I've had to come to terms with over the years, and take responsibility for. Maybe her spoiled behaviour, which we did not do enough to nip in the bud, was a reaction to the pain she tried so hard to hide. Maybe demanding that Yaris was her way of acting out, her form of punishment against us for not seeing what she was hiding in plain sight. But, as I've said, there was also the side to her that was the complete opposite. She could be utterly unselfish.

When we lived in Mayfield, Frances and I had a third musketeer in our gang of mothers: Sheila. She and her children were like part of our families too, but when Frances died, I didn't see Sheila at all. I wasn't able to talk to anyone outside the immediate family for a long time.

A couple of years after Frances passed, Sheila called to see me. She said, 'You know, Collette, after Frances went I had a nervous breakdown.'

I hadn't known a thing about it, and I felt guilty for not being more attentive, although I'd been having my own breakdown, too, of sorts.

'I don't know how Leanne heard about it,' Sheila

said. 'She started calling in to me regularly with flowers. She'd come and sit with me. I can't tell you how much it meant.'

Leanne had never mentioned this to any of us, and when I asked her about it, she said she hadn't wanted to upset me. At the time, any talk of Mayfield and Frances upset me.

Another thing Leanne did, which we didn't hear about, was step in for Frances's children. When Joe went out, the children would be nervous about being left alone, so Leanne would go to Mayfield to stay with them.

She had a lovely way about herself, a kindness that wasn't showy. She didn't do it for praise. Half her clothes were missing from her wardrobe when she died. They'd all been given to various friends. She was constantly giving things away.

The Toyota Yaris was her pride and joy, but it was the source of some awful bullying too. She loved to be out and about in it, giving people lifts here and there. One day she got a call to pick up a certain friend from the car park at Dunnes Stores in the city centre. When she got there, the friend was nowhere to be seen, so Leanne went into Dunnes to see if she could find her.

When she came back, her car was so covered in flour, eggs and milk, you couldn't see a bit of the paintwork or windows. She called Triona, who went down to help her, but the stuff was so thick, the two of them couldn't get it off.

Triona's husband had to leave work to come and drive it to a carwash. Even after it went through three times, they were still scooping the goo out of the engine.

Anthony and I didn't hear about this for a long time. Leanne swore Triona to secrecy because she didn't want us asking questions.

I still think about the girl who phoned Leanne to collect her, that so-called friend. I find it hard to understand how she could have been involved in such wickedness.

When Leanne died, her car was in the garage to be fixed after getting vandalised, the second such incident in the lead up to her death. A gang had laid into it and torn the mirrors off both sides.

I actually saw what they did. I got a phone call from Leanne as I was leaving work and she was sobbing. 'I'm in Mayfield,' she said. 'The car is damaged.'

I thought she'd had a crash and I was worried that she'd hurt herself, but she told me she was all right.

When I got to Mayfield there was a gang of around forty surrounding her car. Leanne was in the middle of them, standing next to it.

I thought, *I'm going to kill her!* I knew nothing about the eggs and flour episode, and my first thought was that she had no respect for the car, the way it was sitting there.

But when I got out, I could hear all these people shouting abuse at her, and she was just standing there with her head down – a lone, vulnerable little figure.

I got into the middle of the crowd, alongside Leanne. 'What's going on?' I asked her.

'They wrecked my car, Mam.'

I looked at the crowd and recognised a lot of the faces in it. I had no idea what these people were doing to Leanne, the torment they were putting her through. I'd thought they were her friends.

'They wanted me to go drinking with them in the field,' Leanne told me.

By this stage, she'd given up going to the field – she was trying to look after herself in that way.

I roared at them, 'In ten years time, you'll all still be in the bloody field!' I can't remember much else of what I yelled, but I do remember that they weren't a bit intimidated. These people didn't have any fear in them. They did exactly what they wanted to do.

I drove her car home with her crying softly in the passenger seat. I did my best to reassure her. 'You know, Leanne, I'm proud of you,' I said. 'You stood on your own two feet there and you didn't go down to the field. You're coming into your own.'

The car cost €800 to be fixed. She collected it from the garage a few weeks later and called us in Lanzarote on Anthony's phone. 'They valeted it and it's like new,' she told her father, all excited.

He handed the phone to me. 'I love you, Mam,' she said, and for the first time ever, I didn't say it back to her. I was cross because she'd stayed in a friend's house on Saturday night and never phoned on Sunday to wish me a happy Mother's Day.

She kept saying, 'I love you, Mam. Come on, say it back.'

Instead, I said that when I came home we were going to have a sit-down and a chat, and that her allowance was going to be cut back.

It was the last thing I ever said to her.

17

When Leanne was small, I'd say to her, 'The school is not going to disappear if you're not there,' because she'd always have to be the first in every morning. That was how much she loved school.

She was a natural leader. I remember at a parent–teacher meeting being told that she would volunteer everybody to do a job, and volunteer herself alongside them. She could get shy people to participate in things and she'd be right there in with them.

Leanne wasn't as academically bright as Triona, but she worked hard and she was well liked by her teachers. When she got her Junior Cert results, one of her teachers was brought to tears: he was so happy for her success. In fifth year she decided she wanted to be a midwife, and she began applying herself to her studies so that she might get the points she needed in the Leaving Cert.

But a few months before she died, Leanne stopped going to school. I couldn't figure it out because she'd always been so dedicated.

One afternoon I was sitting in the kitchen and she was by the cooker, making something to eat. It was a school day and she hadn't gone in.

'Leanne, I want to talk to you,' I said.

Her face shut down. 'Leave me alone, Mam, please.'

'What's going on?' I pleaded. 'If you want to leave school, you can. It's not a problem. I don't care if you're cleaning the roads, once you're happy.'

'Yeah, you'd love that, wouldn't you?' she said.

You can't win with teenagers, but I must have caught her at a vulnerable moment. She pushed her phone across the table towards me without looking up.

I couldn't believe what I saw. Someone had sent a text to her saying she was a whore and a tramp, and that she was after having sex with two boys on top of a washing machine. There was no name to show who the text had come from, only a number.

When I looked at Leanne, tears were streaming down her cheeks.

'Leanne, that's not even possible,' I said. I could barely comprehend what the text had said.

'You don't understand, Mam,' she said. 'All my friends are getting texts saying this about me.'

'Who's sending them?' I asked. 'That's a form of bullying.'

But Leanne's expression shut down again and I couldn't get anything else out of her.

When Anthony came home from work, I told him about the text, and together we went to the school to talk to the acting principal. The school's principal was on a year's leave of absence.

'We have a problem with Leanne,' I explained. 'She's getting texts saying she's a whore and that she's had sex with two guys. Her friends are getting the texts too.'

The impression we were given was that it was out of the school's hands.

Soon after, we managed to persuade Leanne to go back to school, to keep working for her points to study midwifery. A couple of weeks later, she came home distraught. Because of her dyslexia, Leanne had been exempt from studying Irish all through secondary school. When you are exempt, you get a certain amount of discretionary points in lieu of the Irish exam in the Junior and Leaving Certs.

'I've been told I have to do the Irish exam for the Leaving,' Leanne told me.

I was thinking there was a misunderstanding. Leanne was very emotional, so she might have taken the message wrong. So, back to the school Anthony and I went.

The acting principal said, 'Yes, Leanne will have to sit the Irish exam.'

'But she's dyslexic,' I protested, but the acting principal was having none of it.

We paid €300 to have another assessment done, and the result was the same as it had been the first time. Leanne was certified dyslexic. Yet still the acting principal told us she'd have to do her Irish exam.

Another day she came home upset again. 'I've been taken out of honours English,' she said.

I figured she might be struggling with honours, but she told me she'd been moved to the pass class because the honours class was too full.

We went into the school again, where we were told that Leanne would be doing the same work in the pass class as she would in honours. I didn't have any understanding, because I didn't have much schooling, but I knew that something wasn't right.

'If I can't do honours English, I won't be able to get the points I need,' Leanne explained. 'And I won't be able to do the Irish exam.'

I enquired about a private school. We would borrow

from the Credit Union, if that was what it took, but we discovered that Leanne would have to repeat the year. When we put this to her she got very distressed.

'I'm staying at my own school,' she insisted. She sounded tough, but as her diaries would later show, Leanne was battling to stay alive by this stage.

Around this time, too, she had surgery to have her cruciate ligament removed from her knee, which was an operation with very painful recovery time. She'd fallen off a quad bike that she shouldn't have been on, and damaged the ligament. Her whole leg was hugely swollen after the operation, and she couldn't wear her school socks.

The acting principal called me several times about Leanne's socks, insisting that she had to wear them.

Leanne was on crutches during her recovery, and in a lot of pain, so I asked if she could park her car in the teacher's spaces, which were nearer the front door of the school. We were refused.

When I read Leanne's diary, I saw that she was isolated at school, spending more and more time alone in the library. When we were going through her things, we found pages she'd downloaded and printed there, all this religious stuff. I didn't understand much of it – and later we were told by a priest that it was advanced theology – but I did recognise one thing, the psalm that said, 'Though I walk through the valley of death I fear no evil'.

Some of the psalms she printed are for when you're really crying out to God in pain. When I found them, I imagined my little girl crying, like a wounded animal. I reckon she was searching in that library for some peace, because there was none in her life at all.

18

I know I'm drawing a picture of a girl being more and more isolated, pushed further into a corner and, truth be told, she was. But there are all sorts of contradictions to Leanne's story. She had plenty of friends who weren't bullying her, and throughout all of her ordeals she had a boyfriend.

I met him out of the blue one morning when I came downstairs to find a young man asleep on my sofa.

I shook him awake. 'Excuse me, who are you?' I asked.

'I'm Jason,' he replied. 'Leanne's boyfriend.'

'Really?' I said. 'How long are you going out with each other?'

'A few years.' He smiled.

I ran up the stairs to Anthony, who was in bed. 'Leanne's boyfriend is down in the sitting room,' I told him.

'What do you mean, Leanne's boyfriend?'

'He slept here last night.'

Triona knew about Jason, but she wasn't aware how long he and Leanne had been seeing each other. He'd stayed the night, even though Leanne had been pushing him out the door. It was New Year's Eve and he hadn't a chance of getting a taxi, so Triona told Leanne he'd have to stay. All of them had had a few drinks.

Anthony came down the stairs and started giving the poor lad the third degree. I decided to make some breakfast for us all.

Jason was as shocked that we didn't know about him as we were that Leanne had had a boyfriend for a few years. It should have given us some insight into how secretive she was.

He was a very friendly boy, very comfortable with us and chatty. Leanne stormed down the stairs, jangling her car keys. 'Come on, Jason. I'm driving you home,' she told him.

'Wait a minute,' I said. 'I'm cooking his breakfast.'

'Don't start asking him a lot of questions, Mam,' Leanne warned.

'I only asked who he is,' I replied. 'It's not every day you wake up with a strange boy on your couch. Jason, would you like to come to dinner this evening?' I asked him.

'No way,' said Leanne. 'He's going to watch a football match.'

'Yes, I'd love to come for dinner,' Jason said. He had a twinkle in his eye, and you could see he loved winding Leanne up.

She flopped down on the couch and folded her arms. 'You're watching a match,' she insisted.

Jason ended up coming for dinner, but that was the last time he was in our house. I didn't see him again until more than ten years later. I was in a shopping centre with my daughter-in-law – Ant's wife, Debra – and this man almost bumped up against me. 'Sorry, Mrs Wolfe,' he said.

I didn't know who he was, but people often recognise me around Cork, so I said, 'How are you?'

'I'm very good,' he replied, but I could see there was something very sad about him.

'I'm glad to hear it,' I said, and went on my way.

When we got out to the car, Debra said, 'Do you know who that was, Collette? That was Jason Cramer.'

It took the wind out of my sails. I'd read so much about him in Leanne's diaries in the intervening time that I knew how important he'd been in her life. But after she was gone, he seemed to disappear from sight.

'Can you get his number for me?' I asked, so she did a bit of investigating and texted it to me.

I phoned him to tell him I was sorry I hadn't recognised him. When he heard my voice, he started crying.

It wasn't that his life hadn't moved on. He'd had another relationship and a baby boy, but I knew he needed a little bit of closure. I thought about how hard it must have been for him, and for all Leanne's really good friends. She'd left him a ring and a letter.

'Would you like to come over for a cup of tea?' I asked him.

When he came to the house, we both wept. 'I never got the letter,' he told me. 'Triona gave me the ring, but she kept the letter.'

I told him I'd get it for him. 'But I will tell you in the meantime that she wrote a lot about you in her diaries,' I added. 'And there's nothing negative about you. I know you had your ups and downs, but she had great love for you.' I said, 'Jason, make a good life for your son. We don't get a second chance.'

It wasn't easy when I'd heard in the years after Leanne died that Jason had gone into a relationship, or when Leanne's best friend Joanne had a baby. It hurt simply because life goes on, and the people in her life got on with theirs, just as they should.

*

A month or two after we met Jason that New Year's morning, Anthony said he wanted to talk to me.

'I'm a bit concerned about Leanne,' he said.

'Why?' I asked.

'I don't know. I think I saw something in her face. Maybe she needs to talk to somebody. She went through an awful lot with Frances and she was very young at the time.'

Anthony made an appointment for her with a counsellor in a private clinic, and Leanne said she'd go. We knew she liked her privacy and we told her that whatever she said would be between her and the counsellor.

But after her appointment, she refused to go again.

19

The hardest moment to look back on came a few weeks before Leanne's eighteenth birthday, when she was still recovering from her knee surgery. At about nine o'clock one evening she walked in the door. Anthony, Triona and I were in the kitchen, and when we saw her, we couldn't believe our eyes. Her hair was standing up on her head, her face was all cut and bruised, and her clothes were torn and filthy.

'Leanne, what the heck is going on, girl?' I asked.

'Leave me alone,' she said. She burst into tears and ran up to her bedroom.

Triona and I went after her. Her dad knew it was

women's work that had to be done, so he stayed in the kitchen. But he was white as a sheet, his eyes wide as he looked at me.

With the knowledge I gained through reading her diaries, I know she ran up the stairs because she was ashamed to be seen as she was. To me, she looked like a broken little bird.

I was prepared for the worst. She was seventeen, the same age as I was when I was raped and beaten. Triona and I both sat on the end of Leanne's bed. 'What happened?' I asked, as gently as I could. I knew I had to strike a delicate balance to keep her from shutting down. I wanted to hold her, to take her in my arms and soothe the pain she was in, but I couldn't because I knew she'd push me away.

'It was nothing,' Leanne said, trying to make light of it. 'I was heading to my car and these three girls jumped on me. I got to my car and drove off.'

But in her diary the story is different. 'I'm not going to run any more,' she wrote. 'I fighted them the best I could. Knee very sore.'

'Knee very sore.' Even as I write this now, those words are like daggers in my heart. I think of my beautiful girl being beaten and dragged by the hair across the ground, so badly that when I washed it that night, it came out in bunches in my hands. I think of her giving up, of being worn down so hard by her bullies that she just had to accept what was coming.

'Knee very sore.' My baby sounds so exhausted. So helpless. It's written in pencil, that part, and the writing is very childish. It's almost as if she's disappearing as she writes.

Triona and I bathed her. We tucked her up in bed and we told her everything would be okay. But by that stage in her short life, Leanne felt so completely and utterly alone, she couldn't even confide in either of us.

We wanted to get the guards involved, but Leanne begged us not to. As we later found out, she was too afraid. She felt she was never going to get away from her tormentors, that they were never going to leave her alone.

She didn't want a party for her eighteenth, so we decided to go out for a family meal, myself and Anthony, Ant and his girlfriend, Debra, Triona and her partner Edward, and their son, Adam. Leanne didn't mention anything about inviting Jason along.

I remember having to take a step back when she came down the stairs before we went out. She looked so naturally gorgeous, like a butterfly that had emerged from a cocoon. She'd gotten lots of money from my mother, who was so fond of her, and from her uncles and aunts for her birthday, and with it she'd gone out and bought a new outfit for herself.

She wore a beautiful fitted dress, her hair had a

lovely cut, and her make-up was perfect, not too heavy, enhancing her features rather than concealing them. It was like she had regained control of herself after that terrible night. The old Leanne was back, with her infectious laugh and her cockiness.

We went to my mother's house before going to the restaurant, and she was bowled over by how stunning Leanne looked. My brother Martin was there and he said, 'God almighty, she's a beautiful-looking girl.'

'She is,' I agreed. 'And she's mine.'

I was so proud of her and I thought that maybe she'd put behind her the bad experiences at school, the horrible texts and what happened to her the night she was beaten. She seemed completely at home in herself, comfortable and happy.

I was thinking maybe it was time for Anthony and me to step back, that we could start relaxing and have a bit of our own time. We'd booked a week away in Lanzarote, and Leanne had said she didn't want to come, that she'd prefer to stay home and study for her Leaving Cert.

Triona, Edward and Adam had moved out into their own place, and I asked Triona if she'd come to stay with Leanne while we were away, so that she'd have some company. Eighteen was too young for her to be home alone for a whole week.

I remember watching Leanne laugh so easily at that meal, full of bubbly chatter and excitement, and thinking she'd turned a corner, that she was coming into herself as an adult.

Less than two weeks later, Leanne would take a cocktail of pain medication that was in our bathroom cabinet for an injury Anthony had had at work and the back cramps I sometimes suffered from, and die alone in her bedroom.

20

U ya whore on my nans soul u wudnt want ta
bump in ta me any time soon i swear cause im
going ta brake ur face u worse dan da prostitutes.
— text sent to Leanne on 23 March 2007
at 11.19 p.m.

'Leanne is dead.'

Standing inches away from my husband in that
hotel room in Lanzarote, listening as my son said these
words to his father over the phone, I understood that
my life as I knew it was over.

Anthony began to scream. It was a sound like nothing I'd ever heard on this earth. He flung his phone to the floor and it shattered into pieces. I grabbed at his arm, but he pushed me away and bolted towards the balcony door. We were four or five storeys up. I thought he was going to throw himself off.

That terrible fear I'd had as a child came flooding back. It gripped me and I knew I wasn't safe any more. There was no safe place.

I started screaming too, crying at him, 'Anthony! Are you blaming me?'

I don't know why I said that. Maybe I was thinking about how I'd refused to tell Leanne I loved her the last time I ever spoke to her.

Anthony stopped dead in his tracks. 'Blaming you for what?' he asked.

'Because Leanne is gone.'

He shook his head. 'No.' I could see he was struggling to take in what was happening.

'We have to calm down, Anthony,' I said, trying to catch my breath. I still didn't believe what I'd heard. 'We need to find out what's going on.'

I fixed the phone back together, every part of my body shaking. Anthony couldn't function so I put him on the sofa and sat alongside him. 'Hi, Ant,' I said, when my son answered, as if I was beginning a normal phone conversation.

'Mam . . .' my son sobbed. He sounded like a little

boy, crying out for his mother. I could hear Triona howling in the background.

'I need to know what's happening,' I said to my son.

'I don't know,' Ant whimpered. 'Leanne's dead.' He kept repeating it: 'Leanne is dead, Mam. She's dead.'

'Where are you?' I asked.

'I'm in her room. There's guards, paramedics . . . They're after finding a note.'

I remember saying, 'A note about what?'

I still hadn't figured it out. I thought she'd been killed in a car accident, or that she'd been murdered.

'Mam, she's after taking tablets,' my son said.

I couldn't process it. I had never dealt with suicide. But I knew what death was, and I knew by the time I got home I wouldn't recognise my daughter.

So I said to Ant, 'Tell everyone to get out of the room and close the door behind them.'

When they were gone, I asked him to put his phone to Leanne's ear.

I said to her, 'Mammy's on the way home. It's going to be okay. I love you, I'm coming home.'

When Ant came back on the phone, he said, 'They want to take her away. They want to put her into a bag.'

'Who's there with you now?' I asked.

'There's a guard,' he replied.

I said, 'Put him on to me.'

The guard's name was Mark Ryan. 'I'm so sorry for your loss, Mrs Wolfe,' he said.

'Thank you,' I replied. I wasn't crying. I was bringing myself under control. It was the system I'd used when I was eight years old, when I had to get on a bed and have terrible things done to me. I said, 'Mark, my children are devastated. I can't let them see their sister going out of our house in a bag.'

When the guard put me back on to my son, I said, 'The morning coat Frances bought for Leanne is somewhere in her room.'

'It's wrapped around her, Mam.'

'Ask the paramedics will they cover her with that, and with a sheet.'

They were very respectful and did as I asked. I knew what was going on, because Ant stayed on the phone with me as they were taking her out of the house.

Then my son said, 'They're putting Leanne into the back of a van.' He was crying hard. 'It's dark in there, Mam. I can't . . . I can't let them do it.'

'You need to leave her be, Ant,' I said. 'You need to let her go.'

I was on automatic pilot. I was coping. But I couldn't say, 'It will be okay, son, we'll come through this,' because there was no coming through it, not for any of us.

My sister Loretta was there, so I told Ant to put me on to her. 'Bring my children to Mam's,' I told her.

Once word got around, people would start arriving at our house and my children wouldn't be able to cope. I knew that if they got to my mam's place she'd protect them like a guard dog.

When I got off the phone, I didn't know what to do next. I decided to get a taxi to the police station, but when we got there, they didn't know what I was talking about. It was partly because of the language barrier, partly because we were incoherent with shock. The police probably thought we were drunk.

We hailed another taxi for the airport, but the taxi driver said the airport was closed. So we had to go back to the apartment. There, I dialled number after number, trying to get the holiday rep. Eventually when I got through and told her what had happened, she said to meet her in the lobby.

There was a bus for the airport standing outside the hotel. It would be leaving in a couple of hours, but the rep said she'd try and get us a taxi rather than put us on it. She told us to go back to our room and pack.

I put my case on top of the bed, but there was nothing in the room I wanted to bring home. If I could have burned everything I had with me, I would have. All those summer clothes filled me with a violent kind of shame. I'd been on holidays while my child was dying.

I had a camera and I knew there were photographs of her on the film, so I put that in a small bag, along with a pair of shoes I'd bought for her the day we arrived and a bracelet I'd borrowed from her. Everything else I left behind.

The rep couldn't get us a cab, so we had to travel to the airport on the bus. It must have been a hellish journey for the other passengers. We couldn't control ourselves. We weren't crying – we were wailing. Hearing Anthony's cries, my heart nearly jumped out of my chest. I couldn't comfort him: there was nothing I could say.

When we got to the airport all the flights to Ireland were full. The rep tried everything, and eventually she was told that three drunk men had been taken off a plane bound for Dublin and we could have their places.

When the plane took off I had the thought that it could crash, that if it went down I wouldn't have to face what was waiting for me.

I told Anthony that if someone offered him a drink, he was not to take one. I've seen what alcohol does to vulnerable people and I didn't want him disappearing into a bottle. He hadn't said one word since the phone call. He looked like a man coming apart at the seams.

When our plane landed in Dublin, my phone buzzed into life. I hadn't been able to get phone calls or texts on it while we were away.

There was a message from Leanne. 'You are the best parents ever,' she'd written. 'I love you.'

She'd sent it while she was dying.

21

No parent in their wildest nightmares ever imagines they'll be picking out a coffin for their child. Only a few weeks ago we had been picking out a Debs dress for Leanne. It was mind-boggling.

My son tried his best to be helpful. 'What about this one, Mam? That one looks nice.' But I didn't care about any coffin. The words 'death boxes' came into my mind, but I couldn't say what I was thinking. I had to stay in control.

Laid out in the coffin, Leanne was so swollen from the medication she'd taken that she didn't look like herself. Her hair was the only thing that was familiar.

Anthony still hadn't uttered a word. He stood at the top of the coffin stroking Leanne's hair. It was something he'd always done to her, to me and the other children, when we were struggling. It was his effort at reassurance.

I wondered what he was feeling, because I felt nothing. It was as if there was a huge gap inside me, an empty, barren space. I felt that if I touched Leanne in that coffin, I might splinter into a million pieces.

I thought, *I'll never hold you again. I'll never wrap my arms around you. I'll never be able to say to you, 'It's okay, Leanne. You're loved.'*

Triona must have read my mind. She said, 'You can put your hands in underneath her, Mam.'

Triona guided me and I did it, but all I could think was how heavy Leanne felt. How cold. Then thoughts of her autopsy flew through my mind, what they must have done to her. I wanted everyone out of the room so I could search her, so I could see what had happened to my child's body.

I was thinking, *Keep it together, Collette, keep it together. You're not the only one in this.*

I looked at my husband and children and thought, *This family is finished. We're not going to be able to make it through this.*

I needed to get out of that place, so I said to them, 'We'll go back to my mam's now.' We'd gone to my mother's house directly from Cork airport and still hadn't entered our own home. Anthony and I couldn't face it.

Back at my mam's, the whole family was there. Everyone was talking, making sandwiches, coffees and teas. I'd love to say everything was a blur, but it wasn't. I was on high alert. I wanted to hear why my daughter was in a funeral home. There had to be some explanation. How could I have been so blind that I'd missed what was going on, that I'd missed the fact that my daughter wanted to kill herself?

I couldn't swallow any food or drink. I was sitting at my mother's kitchen table because it was the done thing, what you were meant to do. You weren't meant to run out into the road, screaming. You weren't meant to tear the hair out of your own head.

At about ten o'clock that night, we'd decided it was time to go home. When I walked through the front door, the house felt achingly empty, as if all the life had been cut out of it. I couldn't imagine a happy family had ever lived in its rooms.

None of us could sleep that night. The four of us lay on the same bed – myself, Anthony, Triona and Ant, huddled together in our own silent, private horror. My husband and children were wide-eyed with fear.

We had an open coffin at her removal, but at the time I wished we'd left it closed. I wanted people to remember the cheeky grin that lit up her whole face, not the empty shell lying in that box.

So many people came, and I was grateful for it. A crowd of schoolgirls arrived wearing their uniforms, her friends from sixth year. Other friends arrived too, from her days in Mayfield.

As the prayers were being said, out of the corner of my eye I saw Mary 1, the girl who had given Leanne a black eye a few years ago, the one Triona and I had warned to stay away from her. She kept going up to the coffin to look at Leanne.

Under her breath, Triona said to me, 'What's she doing here? She didn't even like Leanne.'

'Stay calm, Triona,' I said, although I wanted to shout at the girl to leave my daughter alone.

Then I saw the undertaker leaning in to whisper something to her. Later I heard he told her that if she went up to the coffin one more time, she'd be asked to leave.

When they cleared the removal, myself, Anthony and the children were given time alone with Leanne. We sat in the front row, not wanting to leave. We knew that when we went they'd close the coffin and we'd never again in this life see her face.

Charlie said we could close the coffin ourselves, if we wanted. I stood up to attempt it, but I thought, *I gave birth to her. There's no way I can shut her into a box.*

Anthony and Ant closed the coffin. I watched as they turned every screw, and I saw how hard it was for them to do it. Anthony was making a choking noise, like he couldn't catch his breath. I knew it was the sound of his heart tearing into pieces.

She was brought to Ballyphehane church, where I'd got married. We had to leave her there overnight in that empty, dark place. I could have kept her at home, but nobody offered that choice, and I was so out of it, it hadn't occurred to me that I could do it. I would have loved that: we could have had a private and intimate time saying goodbye to our girl.

Everyone came back to our house, the whole family. At about four in the morning I said to my mam, 'You need to go home and get rest.'

She said, 'You're *my* child, Collette. I need to see you get some rest.'

I had to lie and tell her we were going to bed. The four of us went up the stairs and lay together in the same bed again, not sleeping. We knew we were facing the funeral, and it would be the hardest day of our lives so far. What we didn't know was that we were about to face another terrible revelation.

22

Triona,

I remember from my birthday card you said, to the world's best sister 'ha', you're my only best friend. I always, and I mean always looked up to you (and Anthony – of course).

I know deep down we were best friends Triona. Things are perfect with you Triona. You have a beautiful son who I cherish like he was my brother.

I want you 2 tell mammy and daddy I wouldn't have chose a better mam & dad. I

idolise my dad, and my mam, what a woman.
Sorry.
Leanne xxxx

– a note left by Leanne to her sister

The morning of the funeral we had to gather things to bring to the altar as mementos of her. Anthony searched the house, turning it upside down. He was looking for his favourite photograph of Leanne, the one of her swimming with the dolphins.

I was in the kitchen, talking to myself. 'Today's the day you're going to be burying your daughter, Collette. After today, things are going to really crumble.'

From above my head I heard Triona let out a howl of pain. I bolted up the stairs, but when I got to the landing I stopped. I didn't believe in God, but I said a kind of prayer. 'Please, don't give me any more to bear.'

In Leanne's room, Triona was sitting on the bed, holding two pages. She was ashen and her hands shook as she cried, 'Mam, they made Leanne's life a living hell!'

She'd found a box of diaries under the bed and at the top were these two pages. She handed them to me and I read the words, 'I want these pages read in front of everyone at my funeral.'

She'd written down names. She'd written about how these people had made her feel. The word 'BULLIES' was in capital letters.

On the night she died, when I spoke to the guard Mark Ryan, he told me there were texts on Leanne's phone and that he had to take it away.

It all began to register with me. Things started falling into place and I knew in my heart and soul that we were going to find terrible things in that box of diaries.

Anthony had come up the stairs without me hearing him. He took the pages from me and read them, tears streaming down his face.

'Give me those pages, Anthony,' I said. I returned them to the box and pushed it back under the bed.

'We have Leanne's funeral to get through,' I told my husband and daughter. 'That's all we can do for now.'

But when we got downstairs, I did one thing. I phoned Mark Ryan and asked him to tell the people Leanne had named to stay away from her funeral.

Then we had to wait until it was time to be collected for the church. I couldn't stay still. I kept looking at the front door, wanting to pull it open and make a run for it, as if I could get away from the terrible truth that soon I would be putting my child into a hole in the ground. The minutes were ticking down. The more I looked at that door, the more I thought I was going to explode.

My brother Martin arrived. He could see the agitated state I was in. 'Come on, Collette,' he said. 'We'll go for a walk.'

We didn't walk far, but it helped me bring things

under control. When we got back to the house the funeral car was parked outside. At the door, Triona and Anthony were in a terrible state of tears and moaning. My son was trying to be the adult, quietly taking care of everything the way he'd learned from his dad, but underneath his black suit I could see that his whole body was trembling.

My poor mother was in the funeral car. She'd been so fond of Leanne. She'd buried two grandchildren, lost two of her own daughters, but she was still so kind and loving. There was no bitterness or hate in her.

I wanted Leanne's coffin to be covered in white roses, like a blanket over her. It was my way of telling her that she was loved unconditionally. It looked beautiful standing in front of the altar, the flowers flowing down the sides to the floor, so that the coffin itself was completely concealed. It was the last thing I could do for her.

I'd asked Ant to go up and say something about his sister, because neither I nor Anthony nor Triona would be able. He did so well, speaking about Leanne, what kind of a person she was and how much she was loved, and I was proud of him.

When he was finished, I put up my hand. Originally I'd thought I wouldn't be able to say anything from the altar. But I couldn't get the pages we'd found out of my head.

I got to my feet. Triona grabbed my wrist and said, 'Don't go up, Mam.'

But I had to.

I'd say everyone was shocked to see me walking up to the altar. I pulled myself together and looked at all the people from every part of our lives who had turned up to give their support. There must have been thousands there.

'When I was flying home from Lanzarote, I couldn't make sense of my daughter being dead,' I said. 'But I make sense of it now. I know why. She's dead because of what other people did to her. She's dead because she was bullied.'

Leanne had hidden her abuse. She'd locked it up and thrown away the key, just as I had all those years ago. She'd blamed herself for it. She'd lived in secret torment and shame.

I didn't know how I was going to get through the rest of my life, never mind the rest of that day, but I did know one thing: I would never live in secrecy again.

23

Ant chose 'She Will Be Loved' by Maroon 5 to be played as Leanne was taken from the church. It was her song: she listened to it all the time when she drove her car, and its lyrics about a girl of eighteen with a broken smile were heart-wrenching to hear. The funeral director, Charlie, came to me and asked if myself and the children would like to stand either side of the coffin and wheel it out of the church, rather than have pallbearers. He knew what a close-knit family we were and that this would feel more fitting for us.

As we walked with the coffin, I could hear people crying throughout the church. It seemed absolutely unreal, as if I was outside myself watching the scene. I'd walked behind the coffins of two sisters and one grandchild, and they were awful grief-stricken experiences, but this was in a whole other realm. Every step I took was towards something I couldn't begin to fathom, that moment when I'd have to walk away from a graveyard where my child was buried and into a life without Leanne.

Outside the church, pallbearers were needed to lift the coffin into the hearse. Anthony, Ant and Edward did it, along with other men from the family. Triona said she wanted to walk underneath the coffin.

'Can you mind Adam?' she asked me.

My grandson stood with his tiny five-year-old hand in mine. 'Nanny, I want to carry her too,' he said.

So I lifted him up and he put his hand on the coffin as it was carried. A picture came into my head of all the times Leanne had taken Adam in her arms. She'd adored him, and he'd adored her in return. She often said that he was more like a little brother than her nephew, and she'd looked out for him the same way an older sibling would. I was so glad I had the strength to lift him so he could carry her now.

As we were being driven to the graveyard, Anthony spoke for the first time.

Triona said, 'Look outside, Mam and Dad. See who's in front of Leanne.'

There was a garda escort leading the hearse. I

know now that Leanne's godmother, Jacinta Malone, organised it – her husband is a guard – but I hadn't a clue at the time that it was going to happen. She'd asked Mark Ryan to help.

'If only Leanne could have seen that,' Triona said. 'She'd have loved it.'

For a moment, a hint of normality returned to Anthony's face. He smiled at Triona and said, 'She would have.' Then he reached out and touched Triona's cheek as if to say, 'I'm still here. I'm still your dad.'

At Kilcully graveyard, where Frances and her daughter are buried, I said I wanted to help carry Leanne. As I shouldered her coffin with my husband and son, memories came flooding back of her birth. Memories of looking at Anthony as he held her and fell instantly head over heels. Memories of cradling her in the hospital bed, taking in her tiny features. I'd wanted her so badly, and for so long, and there she was in my arms, a living, breathing, beautiful thing. Her face wasn't scrunched up like the faces of most newborn infants are, she was open-eyed, alert and ready for life.

I remembered how frightened I became, how terrified I was in those first few weeks that I'd lose her. And now my greatest fear had come to pass. I had lost my little baby.

No matter how they dressed up that hole in the ground with fake grass and wreaths, I thought it was an ugly thing. The priest said a few words and it was time to place her in the grave. Somebody attempted to grab my attention, so I wouldn't see her going down, but I wanted to see it because I felt I deserved everything that was coming to me. The guilt I felt was only a sliver of what would come, but it was enough to have me thinking I'd as much as killed her myself. For what kind of mother wouldn't know her own child was in so much trouble?

My legs started to buckle. How was I going to leave her in that hole? What was going to happen to her?

Triona came to my aid. 'Mam, you told me that you're going to be strong,' she said. I had, but she hadn't understood what I really meant. I was going to be strong as long as Leanne was there. Now I had to leave and I didn't have to be strong any more.

She took my arm and I walked away, never to be near my Leanne again. I knew I could come to the graveyard to visit, but I didn't even like visiting Frances's grave, because I could get no sense of her being there. I couldn't imagine coming back to this awful place and finding any semblance of Leanne.

I looked at my husband as he left the graveyard, bent in two with grief. I thought, *How long are we going to last together? Which one of us is going to die first?* It was only a matter of time, because you can't live without hope. And hope was dead.

At the funeral lunch, I wasn't able to get my foot over the threshold. I stayed outside while Anthony,

Triona and Ant did their best to talk to the people who gathered. After a short while, Anthony came outside too. 'I can't do this any more,' he said.

We went straight to my mam's house. I had gravitated there because I felt like a lost little child myself, in need of my mother. She knew it and she took good care of me, and of all of us. She passed away a year after Leanne, and I look back with gratitude that she was still there to mother me that day. I don't know if I would have survived without her.

In my mam's sitting room, something came over me. I slipped down in the chair, feeling as if I was drifting away. Triona was calling to me, but she sounded far away. There was a kind of peace in it and, for a moment, I thought I was dying.

A doctor was called and I was diagnosed with exhaustion. I was disappointed because I would have welcomed death in that moment. I would have welcomed it as punishment for being the worst mother ever put on this earth. I would have welcomed it because I couldn't imagine how I was going to get through the next minutes, never mind the next days, weeks, months and years. I would have welcomed it, because life had no meaning for me any more.

I didn't know then, as I know now, that a guardian angel had already been sent to help me.

24

F. came up to me screaming and shouting at me. I was so scared. I'm so sick of life I swear. I feel depressed. I wish I had a new life ... I swear World War III is about to happen. I'm so sick of fighting.

The days after the funeral were endless. I spent them staring into space, barely moving, hardly eating. Doing the smallest thing for myself, even making a cup of coffee, felt overwhelmingly selfish. How could I still be alive, still drinking coffee, when my daughter was dead?

At night I'd go to bed and lie awake, the space between Anthony and me a massive, silent gap. I understand now how so many couples eventually split up after losing a child. We couldn't hold each other. We could scarcely look at each other. I think it was because neither of us felt we deserved comfort.

He'd receded into silence and it was as if I was watching the man I loved disappear before my eyes. I could see he was torturing himself, but didn't know how to reach out to him. I didn't know if I'd ever be able to reach out to him again. It felt like the marriage I'd known was as dead and gone as Leanne.

In the morning my day would start all over again. The pain felt like nothing I had ever known. It was as if I'd been given open-heart surgery with no anaesthetic.

My fear grew. I became sure I was going to lose one of my other children to suicide.

Ant had been a paragon of strength in the lead-up to and during the funeral, but he was beginning to fall apart. You'd always say of Ant that he couldn't pass a mirror without taking a look at himself. He takes good care of his body, getting proper exercise and eating well, and he always dresses as if he has something important to do. In the days after Leanne was buried he seemed to close in on himself and shrink, the handsome, well-presented young man disappearing, leaving a shell in his wake. He wouldn't speak about Leanne to me, or to anyone.

Triona was the opposite. She stayed up for two nights reading the diaries, like a detective trying to piece together a crime. I could see that every word was turning into a blade to lacerate her. She couldn't believe she hadn't known what was going on, that she hadn't been able to help her sister.

I remembered her telling me she was sorry over and over again the night we got home from Lanzarote.

She was the one who found Leanne. That day when she came home from work, Leanne's car was in the driveway. Upstairs, she looked in on her sister, who seemed to be asleep. Then later in the evening, when Leanne was still in her bedroom, she'd hovered outside the door. She could hear what sounded like snoring, so she went to bed herself, thinking Leanne must be exhausted because she'd been out late the night before. My poor Triona had been in the house, sleeping in the next room, while Leanne took her last breaths. I thought it was something she'd never get over.

I couldn't bear to go into Leanne's room, never mind read her diaries. I knew I had to eventually, that there was no getting away from them, but I didn't know how to begin. Anthony wasn't emotionally equipped to read them either.

The question I was afraid to ask was: am I in there?

I wanted ten pages about how much she loved her mam and how good her mam was. I wanted absolution from my guilt, but I was terrified the pages would be filled with the reasons for it. All the clashes we had over the amount of pocket money she was going through, all the fights over what she was wearing – ironically I wanted her to wear clothes that showed off her beauty rather than the shapeless sweatshirts she wore to hide herself – all the times I'd grounded her. The fact that I hadn't said I loved her the last time I spoke to her.

Expecting the worst, I sat Triona down and asked if Leanne had written anything bad about me. 'No, Mam, there's not much about you at all. But she was in a very bad way. There were an awful lot of bullies and they really hurt her.'

One morning Triona came to me in the kitchen and said, 'I'm having a terrible dream, Mam. I wake up every night and Leanne is under the bed. I take her out to see if she's okay, and then I put her back underneath again.'

To reassure her, I said, 'Maybe you're trying to keep her safe, Triona.' But the fear of God filled my heart. I thought, *There's no way my children are going to survive this. There's no way any of us are. I have to get some help.*

There was nobody knocking at the door, no priest or social worker asking if we needed help. Our daughter and sister had taken her own life: the authorities had been involved in the immediate aftermath, but then we were left to our own devices. Anthony's niece Sonya, had given me an envelope with €300 in it. I decided I was going to pay for counselling with it.

I searched through the phonebook and found a woman. I called her and made an appointment, and the four of us got in the car to drive to her office.

Afterwards Triona, who always kept her sense of humour, said, 'My God! Dad was driving so slowly, it took us about twelve months to get to that counsellor.'

Poor Anthony was struggling through every day, like he was trudging through mud, unable to speed up. By comparison our Triona was a fast driver, the kind who would have you clutching and braking in the passenger seat.

When we arrived, my son said, 'I'm not going in.'

I said, 'You are, Ant. If I have to kick you through the door, you are.'

To begin with the counsellor said she'd meet myself and Anthony while the children waited outside her office.

We explained that our eighteen-year-old daughter had taken her own life, and that we'd found diaries, which detailed a lot of bullying. The counsellor told us she wouldn't be equipped to help us, so we all had to leave.

Mark Ryan, the guard who had spoken to me on the phone the night Leanne's body was found, had taken to arriving at our house after his shift, and that night he called again. His squad car would be parked outside our house so often I'd say the neighbours thought we were drug dealers.

He'd sit in our kitchen in his uniform and chat to us, asking if we were okay or if we needed anything. He'd listen and then he'd leave. My experience with the guards was that they came around when something was wrong, or if something bad was about to come your way.

I didn't understand it. Why was he calling?

25

Today is Tuesday and I'm still depressed as ever. I can't cope with being me. Everyone thinks I'm a tramp and I love the way everyone believes everything they hear ...

Mary 2 wants to ball me. She actually hates my guts, and I'd say if she had the chance, she would rip them out.

L. texted me last night saying that somebody said it to him that I'm a tramp, so I snapped

on him. I love the way everyone's talking
about me ...
The next few weeks are going to be tough for
me. I don't know if I'm going to get through
them.

In the first months after my sister Frances died, I regularly forgot she was gone. I'd expect her to call around or be at the other end of the phone, and then would come the awful realisation that I'd never see her again. It was different with Leanne. The wound she left behind was so open and aching, I couldn't forget.

My daughter's suicide was a knife that sliced my life in two, into Before and After. Before, we'd been a close family, a tight little unit with our own struggles and successes, our joys and sorrows. After, it was like we were shipwrecked, each of us trying to grab on to something to stay afloat, but drifting away from each other and ready to go under at any moment.

I couldn't even look back on that close little unit without thinking it was all a lie. We'd seemed to share our troubles, to be there for each other, but that wasn't true. One of us had been so alone, so unable to reveal her sadness and torment, that she'd decided to leave in the most drastic way possible.

A few weeks after we'd gone to the counsellor who turned us away, my niece Jessica called with a number somebody had given her for a HSE counselling service.

I called it and got through to someone who put us on a priority list. I was told that myself and Anthony could have one counsellor and our children could see another.

This time Ant point blank refused to go. I was worried sick about him. His girlfriend, Debra, was worried, too, and we both asked him to reconsider. But he was adamant, and I thought I understood why. He didn't want to relive the trauma of the night Leanne was found, even though in his mind I knew he was still pitched right in the middle of it. What I didn't know was that, like Triona, like myself and Anthony, he, too, had found a reason to blame himself for Leanne's death.

Triona went to see the HSE counsellor once. Afterwards, she said, 'I'm sorry, Mam, I just can't do it.' It was too soon for her to open up, and for Ant, too. They were still so raw, and the counselling was like pouring acid on their injuries. But I'm the kind of person who always strikes while the iron's hot. The distance between Anthony and me was growing with every day that passed. The only talk that went between us was what had to be said to get through the everyday things. There was no other communication, no mention of Leanne, no talk of our feelings or recriminations. I felt that if my marriage was to be saved, we needed intervention and we needed it quickly.

Our counsellor's name was Eleanor. At our first

meeting, Anthony didn't say much. I, on the other hand, couldn't stop talking. I took her step by step through that night in Lanzarote, through my confusion, my worries for Ant and Triona, my guilt and shame, my constant sense of fear. I took out Leanne's diaries and said that neither Anthony nor I had been able to read them yet. I told her I needed to know what was in their pages.

Eleanor suggested that we give her the diaries and that, once she'd read them, she'd go through them with us, step by step.

At our next appointment, Eleanor told us she'd cried reading the diaries. Then she'd phoned a detective friend of hers to ask if an investigation had been launched into the bullying of Leanne. I remember thinking, *In the name of God, what's in those pages?*

I was afraid that Triona had gone softly, saying there wasn't much in there about me. I expected Eleanor to tell me, 'Your daughter was very angry at you.' I thought I should speak about the fact that I hadn't said I loved her on the last night of her life, when I could and should have, but I felt so guilt-ridden that I couldn't open my mouth to let it out.

Eleanor didn't mention anything about Leanne being angry with me. Instead she told us that we'd go through the diaries one session at a time, that we'd talk about their contents and that Anthony and I would go home then and read the pages we'd just gone over.

The earlier diaries from 2003 are almost entirely about boys Leanne thought she was in love with, who, she worried, didn't feel the same way. She'd kiss some guy and instantly fall head over heels in love with him, and then she'd be distraught because he'd have kissed someone else. Anthony would get exasperated when we were reading these bits. 'She's heartbroken over some boy she's only after knowing a few weeks?' He couldn't fathom it.

'She's a fourteen-year-old girl, Anthony,' I'd tell him. 'That's what all teenage girls are like.'

But part of me didn't recognise the endless agonising over nothing. It didn't tie in with the Leanne I'd thought I knew. I'd pegged her as more mature than that.

There was an element of comfort when we were reading the early diaries. In a way it was like bringing her back to life. They were so full of youth and energy, scrawled with love hearts and 'Leanne loves so-and-so' or 'Leanne and so-and-so 4ever'. There was always some fresh intrigue, a different boy to fixate on, a new plan to 'meet' someone.

There is some negativity about me. Lines here and there, like 'All me and my mam do is fight. I actually hate her so much.' (This was written when we were on holidays in Portugal when she was fourteen.) Or 'Me and mam had a huge fight over the usual. MONEY!'

Reading these lines for the first time wasn't easy. It was painful to think about her being angry with me.

We *did* fight about pocket money, and about curfews, and the usual things mothers and teenagers get into arguments about. But the mentions of our fights were so few and far between, I understood they hadn't been the actual cause of her unhappiness.

The first mention of bullying is in July 2004, when she writes of boys in the Mayfield gang calling her fat: 'I'm so fat, I don't need him telling me. I don't know why all the boys are getting involved. I'm even staying in home over them and I'm making myself sick. I'm staying away from chips. I'll prove them wrong.'

Then there is the first threat that Leanne will be attacked by other girls. '[Mary 1] is getting [Mary 2] after me,' she writes later that July, and then a few days later, 'I feel so depressed, I wish I had a new life.' After that, the bullying just grew and grew.

There are more pages about boys, and as time went on, they centred more on the dramas of her relationship with Jason, but interspersed were pages in which she detailed the latest attack, the names she'd been called, the fear of being beaten again.

Sometimes we'd find ourselves laughing through our horror, at Leanne's typically cheeky way of going on: on 31 August 2005, she writes, 'Sure me and G. are still fighting since that time she wanted to fight me outside McDonald's. Dat was in June like, it's been ages, but I really couldn't care now. She's only a muppet anyway.'

A really hard part of the diaries to read was about how much trouble Leanne got into when she drank. There was a big drinking culture among her friends that we knew nothing about.

She writes about not being able to control herself on drink, and kissing guys she shouldn't be kissing, like someone else's boyfriend, or someone on the side while she's seeing Jason. Much of the bullying stems from this behaviour. She kisses some fella, word gets around, and next thing she's being called a slut.

She doesn't mention it in the diaries, but we discovered later that around that time she was being bombarded with texts telling her she was a whore and a tramp, that she was fat, and that 'they' were going to get her.

And all the time, Leanne was becoming more and more isolated. At the end of September 2005, she writes, 'I have absolutely nobody to talk to, it's just me and all I'm starting to do is isolate myself by not even going out or anything. I don't even have the energy.'

To our terrible shock, we learned that only six months later she made her first suicide attempt.

26

Everyone in the gang thinks I'm a slut, and I'm not, like. There is going to be war then between me and [Mary 2]. I'm wearing a tracksuit today 'cause I know I'm going to be fighting ... If she's going to fight me, then I'm not going to walk away.

I tried to kill myself last night and I didn't succeed because trying to strangle yourself is very hard. So if there's war now today, then

I'm going to overdose. I actually don't care.
I hate me and I don't think I can live with
myself.

How do you put into words what it feels like to learn that your daughter tried to strangle herself but didn't succeed because it was too difficult, and what it's like to imagine the violence of it and the desolation she felt to do something so horrific to herself? And all the time I'd thought she was a normal teenager, living a normal adolescent life. Staying out too late with her friends, worrying over spots, trying out new diets, arguing with Anthony and me over the rules we made, cajoling her brother into giving her extra pocket money so she could have some treat or other, worrying about homework, arguing with her sister over make-up and clothes, giggling with us all over something we saw on Saturday-night TV, hanging around the house at the weekend in her pyjamas and slippers, chatting away to me about this and that, making me laugh with her wicked sense of humour. That was my Leanne, not the child upstairs (for I assume it was in our house) attempting to hang herself.

I could hardly take in any more, but still we continued. Another few pages into the darkness of our daughter's hidden life, then another few the following week. After the counselling sessions we'd read the pages together in silence, each of us trying to make sense of the girl writing those words as opposed to the girl we'd thought we knew.

By the session when we got to where Leanne writes: 'I fighted them the best I could. Knee very sore', Anthony and I were like two shadows, moving through a different world from the one everyone else lived in. It was as if we'd opened a door and entered the terror and loneliness of Leanne's last few months of life, leaving everything else behind. Even Ant and Triona seemed far away.

'Knee very sore.' She'd written this in pencil, Eleanor said, because in some way Leanne had regressed to being a little girl. The word 'fighted' was like something a six-year-old might say, rather than a seventeen-year-old.

As soon as we got home that day, we sat in the front room and read those lines again. 'I fighted them the best I could. Knee very sore.'

I remembered that night, the scratches on her face, her torn clothes, her hair coming out in clumps. I imagined what she must have felt as those girls dragged her along the ground.

That night she'd tried to make light of it, so that I wouldn't know. Why had she kept so silent? I looked back on my own childhood and found the answer. She'd said nothing for the same reason I'd said nothing. She'd thought she deserved it.

I suddenly felt violently ill. I had to run to the bathroom to throw up, my head spinning with recriminations as I hung over the toilet bowl. When I was a child, part of me wished my torment might be noticed. Leanne must have wished the same.

By the time I came back downstairs, Anthony was like something deranged. His eyes were burning and he was making a new noise, one that sounded like a raging animal.

He ran out to the shed and started putting things in the back of his van. A hammer. A saw. A rope. A hatchet.

I knew he was planning to kill them. Part of me didn't care. I wanted those people hurt. I wanted them to know the pain they'd put Leanne through. I wanted their parents to feel the way I felt.

Triona, arriving home from work, came upon the scene. She pleaded with him not to do anything. 'You'll get arrested!' she cried. 'You'll be sent to prison!'

I had witnessed Anthony in a rage a few times before, but I'd never seen anything like this. His hair was standing on end. He was literally wild-eyed. Triona begged him to calm down and see sense, but it was as if he couldn't hear her above the storm in his head. I had a horrible feeling at the pit of my stomach. He was going to do something he'd never be able to come back from.

The doorbell rang and, as if he'd been waiting outside for his moment, Mark Ryan appeared in full uniform.

'How is everyone tonight?' he said, as Anthony dashed past him, carrying a shovel.

Triona stood helpless, crying hysterically. I slumped down at the kitchen table and began to weep too.

Mark went to the kitchen and filled the kettle to make himself a cup of coffee. He took a seat opposite me. 'I read the diaries,' he said. 'I know about what happened to your daughter.'

I gawked at him, this stranger in a uniform sitting at my kitchen table, and bawled. I didn't mind that he'd read my daughter's secret diaries, which I learned Triona had given him. From the moment I'd spoken to Mark Ryan on the phone that night in Lanzarote, I knew he was a decent sort.

In the past few weeks, he was a presence in the house we were almost coming to rely upon. Every day was like a year and the only break seemed to be when Mark came. He wasn't part of our immediate or extended family; he wasn't mixed up in the complications of our grief. He seemed simply to be a witness to what we were all going through.

I found myself looking forward to him calling. I was able to relax in his presence. I found that I didn't have to be any way other than I was, which was a blubbering mess. What you saw was what you got with him, too: there was no other face to him.

'He's going to murder them,' I cried. 'You have to stop him.'

Anthony came in then. 'Don't say a word,' he warned Mark. 'Tonight, I don't care what's going to happen.'

'Where are you going?' Mark asked nonetheless.

'Up to Mayfield. I want answers.'

'Well, you'd want to be careful,' Mark said, leaning back in his seat. 'My advice would be to wear a balaclava. And cover your number plates. Otherwise you'll be recognised.'

I couldn't believe my ears. 'What kind of advice is that?' I asked. 'Aren't you supposed to be a guard?'

'I am,' Mark replied. 'But I'm a father too.'

I realised what he was trying to do – defuse the situation with a bit of humour and with sympathy at the same time. Out of the blue, I found myself laughing at the absurdity of it, this guard in full uniform telling my husband to wear a balaclava.

Anthony stopped in his tracks. The wind went out of his sails and he had to sit down. 'They did terrible things to her,' he said, his face scrunched up with anguish. 'I can't let them away with it.'

Mark nodded. He didn't try to dissuade Anthony or reason with him. He just sat and listened as Anthony spoke about what we'd read, about how he hadn't been able to protect Leanne while she was alive.

'I don't know what to do.' My husband sobbed, his head in his hands. 'What am I supposed to do?'

I knew how he felt. All the time we believed we should be doing something to make this right, as if some bargain could be struck and our pain would go away. Get counselling, read the diaries, try to understand what was going on, get to the bullies, show them that we knew what they did, make them pay, and somehow the horror might be cancelled out. Somehow it might all never have happened and we'd have Leanne back. It sounds crazy, but that's what we were doing – bargaining for our daughter's return.

Mark stayed for an hour or so, listening but not saying very much. He hadn't lost a child to suicide, but there was something about him: he seemed to understand what we were going through. In fact, I knew very little about his life, except that he was the guard who had turned up the night Leanne had died, and hadn't stopped turning up since. I didn't ask him anything that particular night, but curiosity was set off in me about who this man was when he wasn't in our house.

Anthony calmed down, and eventually the van was emptied, all the tools he was going to use to wreak his revenge put back in the shed. That night, I tried to comfort him, to reach out across the void in our bed.

'Collette,' he said, in the darkness. 'I hate those people for what they did.'

'I know,' I said. That part hadn't come for me yet, the anger, but it would. And when it did, it would come with a vengeance.

27

Two weeks after Leanne's death, we discovered that Triona was pregnant. I'd love to say it was happy news, a new life coming into the world to give us a glimmer of hope in the darkness, but it only added to my concerns. My mind kept running over worst-case scenarios, out of control with fear. My old anxieties about losing Leanne as an infant came back ten-fold. Now I started living in terror of the pregnancy killing Triona.

Triona's husband, Edward, was not managing well either. It's strange how tragedy can give you insight into how people really are.

The day after Anthony's murderous episode, Edward
was staying with us. He's a big, tall specimen, Edward
– Triona only comes up to his shoulder – and he looks
like nothing would put the frighteners on him. That
night I found him curled up on the couch, with a quilt
pulled up to his eyes. They looked petrified.

'Edward, what's wrong?' I said. I could see that he
was trembling under the quilt.

'I'm afraid that if Leanne comes back, I'll see her,' he
said, and started crying.

'If Leanne appears to anyone, it'll be to me,' I said.
'Now, go on up to bed.'

Upstairs I told Anthony about Edward's fear. 'If
Leanne does come back, she'll definitely come for that
fella now, to scare him out of his wits,' I said, and the
two of us found ourselves laughing so hard that tears
poured out of our eyes.

It was the strangest feeling, to be laughing at
Leanne's mischievousness after what we'd read over
the past few weeks. I felt guilty to be laughing, but at
the same time it felt right. What she'd written in her
diaries, the shame and sadness she'd hidden, wasn't the
whole of Leanne. The way she'd died wasn't the whole
of Leanne either. It didn't cancel out all the other parts
of her, all the funny, joyful parts of her.

We laughed about Leanne scaring the pants off
Edward, but that night Edward showed me his soft
belly. He showed me there was more to him than

this lads' lad I was always giving out to. Things have changed so much since then. Edward doesn't drink any more. He does Iron Man competitions and triathlons, and he's turned into a good, solid husband and father.

One night, not long after this, Mark Ryan was on one of his visits. He was sitting at the kitchen table with a cup of coffee Anthony had made. I don't remember exactly what I was talking about, but I was in a state.

Out of nowhere, Mark asked, 'Do you blame God for what happened, Collette?'

'I have nothing against God, because I don't think God exists,' I said. 'I'm angry at myself.'

I looked at him through new eyes, the reason for his presence beginning to make itself known. 'What are you?' I asked.

'What do you mean?'

'Are you a Jehovah's Witness, or maybe one of those Mormons?'

'I'm a Christian,' Mark said.

'What's a Christian?' I asked.

'Well,' he said, 'we dress up in black cloaks and we light a fire on top of a hill in the moonlight, and we dance around it.'

I couldn't believe my ears. 'Well, whatever tickles your fancy,' I said, thinking it was probably time for him to leave.

'Collette!' Mark laughed. 'Where's your sense of humour?'

'It's up in Kilcully graveyard,' I replied.

Then Mark got serious. 'You know God loves you, Collette, don't you?' he said.

I couldn't take this. 'Really?' I said. 'If this is love, imagine if God hated me.'

Anthony was very quiet, listening to this conversation, but he'd moved in closer.

'So you believe in all that?' I said to Mark.

'I do,' he replied. 'I believe in Jesus Christ, the Son of God.'

I began to feel very uncomfortable. I didn't know much about this man, and here he was, saying, 'God loves you, Collette.'

I thought, *This man really doesn't have a clue. I'll show him.*

And then as if it had been waiting for this very moment, my whole story tumbled out. I told Mark about the little white mouse, and what happened to me on that bed the first time. I told him about being raped a few days later. I told him about being called a dirty bitch when I was just eight years old.

I couldn't stop talking. I said things I'd never even dared to say to myself. I told him about the man who raped me when I was seventeen, about the way he beat me and my belief that I deserved it.

I told him every detail because I didn't care any

more. The worst thing possible had happened to me. I had nothing left to lose. Keeping secrets hadn't done me or my family any good. Keeping secrets had cost Leanne her life.

As I spoke, I could see understanding dawning on Anthony's face. I'd told him sketchy details about the abuse over the years, but he was hearing most of this for the first time. I didn't stop to ask if he was okay, or to comfort him. I just poured it all out, and when I was finished I felt an enormous sense of relief, as if I'd taken off a straitjacket and my body was free again.

I said I didn't believe in a God that could let that happen to a child. I said I didn't believe in a God that could let what happened to Leanne happen.

Once I'd finished there was silence at the table, and suddenly I didn't know why I'd let it all out. Anthony looked miserable, and I thought, *Oh, no, I've just added a thousand more weights to his shoulders.*

I saw the two men exchange a look, and then Anthony said, 'Sure you could write a book, Collette. It'd be like *Angela's Ashes*.'

'*Angela's Ashes* would be a comedy next to this one,' Mark replied, and suddenly we were all laughing.

It felt like a form of craziness, this blurting out of my story to a man I knew nothing about, the laughing and crying, and in truth I was caught up in a kind of madness. I didn't know what was coming next, what would be revealed, how I'd react, what I would say.

After that Mark drank his coffee and chatted away about other things with Anthony, then said, 'I'm off.'

I remember watching him go out the door and thinking, *We won't see him again.* I'd figured I'd driven a friend away.

As usual Anthony and I didn't sleep that night. He didn't say anything about what I'd come out with at the kitchen table, about the awful things I'd given him to imagine, but I could feel his presence beside me in the bed and it was reassuring. I remembered him as such a young man, barely seventeen himself, turning up at my mam's house with flowers after he'd heard on the Cork grapevine that I'd been raped. He'd sat quietly beside me that day, too, saying nothing.

I'd worried that Leanne's secrets might tear our marriage apart. Ironically, after revealing mine, I thought it had a chance at survival.

28

Two nights later – to my surprise – Mark Ryan was at our kitchen table again, chatting about this and that. Then, in what I would come to see as his usual way of moving from casual conversation to the serious stuff, with you barely noticing it, he started talking about his wife Lorna, and how she'd been severely bullied as a young girl. He said that she'd kept closed about it. In a way, I think he was saying it's normal: we keep secret the things that make us feel different because we want to fit in, because we want to be loved.

It's very sad to think of Leanne keeping her secrets because she wanted to be loved, but I did understand it. I'd thought that if I told anyone about my abuse, I'd be vilified and rejected, so to keep it secret was a way of staying loved. Of course we wouldn't have rejected Leanne for what was happening to her, but who knows what goes on in the mind? She was trapped, I do know that, and she thought it would never end. Maybe the silence was a trap in itself.

Mark had mentioned his wife, Lorna, and it was the first time I got any insight into his life. Now that I had the bone, I was like a dog. I started asking him about the rest of his family.

He told me a story about his son, Jack, who was born prematurely and put on life support. Things were bad. He couldn't have any bowel movements so they said his bowel was going to turn gangrenous. They were giving him morphine for the pain he was in. The doctors said it would be better to turn off the life-support machine. But Mark and Lorna would not let them do it, because they believed that if God wanted to take him He would do it in His own time.

One night Jack was restless. The nurse looked at looked at Jack's notes and saw that he'd been given morphine so he shouldn't have been moving. She was angry with Mark and Lorna, saying, 'Do you realise your child is in terrible pain?'

As she was speaking a light landed directly on Jack's incubator. It couldn't have been from a car or anything on the street because they were three storeys up. Then

Lorna saw a hand being laid on her baby. She knew in that moment that it was God's hand, and that Jack was going to be okay.

Jack survived. He has cerebral palsy and a lot of complications, but Mark said he was a happy boy and that he'd made a lot of progress.

I didn't know what to make of his story about God's hand, and I thought back to his question to me a couple of nights previously: 'Do you blame God for what happened?'

'Did you blame God for what happened to Jack?' I asked.

Mark said that he believed God loved Jack and that God loved me too.

I wasn't convinced because I didn't believe God existed or that miracles like that could happen. But something else became clear to me. Mark was here supporting us because he'd walked a hard road, too. He knew what it was to feel pain over what happened to your child. He understood.

'Would you like to meet Jack?' Mark asked me.

'I would,' I said, and Mark asked me to visit him and his family the next day.

Anthony was shocked. Neither of us had been able to leave the house since Leanne's funeral, not even to go up to my mam's.

'Why are you going?' he asked me.

I told him I wanted to see the truth for myself. It was

fine having Mark come into my home and talk about our lives, but I wanted to see his life with my own eyes. He talked about his God loving him and I wanted to see if this man was walking the way he talked.

What I learned was that Mark, Lorna and their family faced mountains on a daily basis. They watched their youngest son battle with infections, deal with all sorts of physical difficulties any human being would be knocked down dead by. There were times when his bones would have to be broken so he could stretch his limbs, and yet this child was an incredibly happy boy. The feeling I had when I met him is hard to describe. I was almost blown away by what I can only call his grace. The doctors had said Jack would never walk, but Mark and Lorna worked with him every day and had faith that he would, and by the time I met him he was walking.

No one in Mark's family had an easy life, but their house was full of a gentle sense of love and respect. Jack had no hesitation in telling me from the moment I met him that he loved Jesus.

I believed he did. I just didn't believe in Jesus myself. It was good to meet the Ryans, and Mark kept up his visits, just coming in for a cup of coffee in the evenings, passing the time of day. Like me, I could see that Anthony and Triona were coming to rely on his visits too. One night he asked if we would like him to pray for us.

I threw my eyes up to Heaven, and said, 'Knock yourself out, Mark.' I thought it might make him happy. I didn't expect to feel what I felt when he said, 'Father, help these people. Give them some peace in the storm. I'm asking you, God, give them healing, give them comfort.'

I burst into tears, not because I was moved by his words to believe in God, but because I thought this man believed in something that didn't exist.

The days were going on and on. Leanne was gone five months now, and I was on a downward spiral. I thought nothing could help me. Not even the God Mark prayed to.

29

Email from Triona Wolfe to *The Neil Prendeville Show*, 96fm, 27 April 2007

Good Morning Neil,

I am just emailing you in relation to the issues regarding suicide that have been discussed over the past week. Unfortunately I can say that recently my family has been touched by this very painful situation. I was going to ring but I know I wouldn't be able to compose myself properly on the radio.

I will start by telling you what happened. On the 23rd of March 2007 I came home late from work. My sister

Leanne's car was outside so I knew she was at home. When I got in the lights were all off so I went and checked where she was. She was asleep in bed. Snoring actually.

I decided to leave her alone as she was out late the night before. And I thought that since she was in such a deep sleep I couldn't have the heart to wake her. I went into my own room for about two hours and my partner woke me. I went to go downstairs and get a drink of water. When I got to the stairs I noticed her room was silent. Was she still there?

I turned on her light. I don't know what made me think it, but I knew something was wrong. I called her name, no answer! I shook her, no movement! I then turned her over and I knew she was gone.

All I can remember are the screams! It was the last thing we as a family ever thought would happen to us. I had to contact my brother who lives across the way from us to tell him. His world has come down around him. He adores my sister. She is the baby in the family, 18 since the 10th of March.

My parents were on holiday in Lanzarote for a week. My brother had to do the unspeakable task of ringing them to tell them what had happened.

Since then our lives have passed us by in a blur. We are still coming to terms with her being gone, so it's very difficult to try and understand that she accidentally took her own life.

My sister, a beautiful person inside and out, who went around without a care in the world. Who got everything she wanted off my parents. We believe it was a cry for help.

On the morning of my sister's funeral I was searching in her room, I didn't know what for, anything really, an answer even. What I found was much worse. Diaries since 2003. My sister was so unhappy she wrote it all down for years. We never knew it. We lived in each other's pockets and talked to each other every day and we never knew how much she was hurting.

My sister was bullied by a person who is the same age as her and hung around in the same group. She terrorised my sister physically and mentally. She assaulted her in front of all her friends and even gave her a black eye. She got other girls after my sister who tore bunches of her hair out.

We wanted to go to the guards but my sister wouldn't let us. We thought it was sorted after but on reading her diaries where her deepest thoughts are kept, it went on for years. Her bullies told people my sister was a slut and a whore. They were so hurtful to her.

We have gotten a professional to look at my sister's diaries and she couldn't believe how emotionally intelligent my sister is. She couldn't say it out, she had to write it down …

Now we have to try and live without her. It breaks my heart to look at my parents. Their lives are over. They are such good parents and I know that they are now questioning that. They gave us everything, not just materialistically but emotionally as well. I feel heartbroken. I feel a piece of me has died with her and I know they feel a thousand times worse.

My brother has been brought to his knees. We have had all normality and security ripped from us. My parents have been robbed of a daughter that was everything they lived for. The last of the savings. Daddy's little girl. A sister who was so thoughtful in everything she did and a fantastic auntie to her two nephews who adore her and cannot understand that she is gone ...

I hope no other family will ever have to go through what we now have to call a life. I'm sorry for going on, but I just have so much to say and we as a family have so many questions that will never be answered. I hope you take the time to read this.

Thank you.

Triona Wolfe

During Frances's illness, she once said to me that she was like that woman in the water who looked as if she was waving when she was really drowning. In the months following Leanne's funeral I could barely make it to the surface to wave. I had sunk to the lowest depths I had ever known.

While Anthony, Triona and Ant went back to work, trying to get a semblance of a life, I stayed in the house alone, unable to do anything at all. I couldn't watch television or listen to the radio: the images and sounds of people getting on with their lives were unbearable to me. If an alarm went off in a house on our street, the noise was like a drill through my skull. Even the sound of a kettle coming to the boil was excruciating. I couldn't look at the Internet or cook a meal. I'd lost the ability to drive a car, and couldn't even open the curtains on my windows to look outside.

Every time my phone rang, my stomach went sideways. I'd be catapulted back to the hotel room in Lanzarote, to the moment before my world had fallen apart, and I'd be sure this call was to tell me an even worse thing had happened.

On a morning about seven weeks after Leanne's death my phone rang and Triona's name came up on the screen. I watched it ringing for a bit before picking it up, so sure was I that she was calling with catastrophic news. And in line with my fears, when I answered Triona was hysterically crying at the other end of the line.

'I've done something, Mam,' she bawled. 'You're going to kill me.'

'First of all, calm down,' I said, catching control of myself the way I had trained myself to do. 'Then tell me in your own time.'

'The radio was on at work all morning,' she explained. 'Neil Prendeville's show. It was about suicide, Mam, and there were all these callers on saying how selfish it was that these people make their own choices and destroy their families' lives, and that we should have no sympathy for them.'

As I listened, I thought how painful it was for Triona

to hear that while everyone in her office was listening, too, knowing she'd lost her sister to suicide.

Triona went quiet and I could sense she was contemplating whether or not to tell me something more.

'Mam,' she said eventually, 'there's a rumour going around that Leanne took her own life in the field.'

'Listen, Triona,' I replied, 'I don't care about any rumours. We know where Leanne ended her life.'

'But, Mam, I don't want anyone thinking she was in the field. It's not right.'

'What did you do, Triona?' I asked, a feeling of dread making itself known in the pit of my stomach. She'd opened the phone call telling me I was going to kill her because she'd done something.

'I sent an email to the radio show, saying what really happened. Neil Prendeville is going to read it out and he wants me to come and talk about Leanne.'

I knew Triona was in no fit state to talk on the radio. She could barely get out what she had to say to me.

'I can't do it, Mam,' she confirmed, then paused for a second. 'Would you go on instead?'

My first answer was an absolute no. I was barely able to move out of my seat. How would I go on a radio show? 'Are you out of your mind?' I asked my daughter. 'There's not a snowball's chance in Hell.'

'I've not asked you for anything, Mam, not since Leanne died, but I'm begging you to do this. Please.'

I couldn't refuse her. I knew that she needed her only sister to be remembered for who she was, not some out-of-control teenager who allegedly killed herself in a place where gangs went to drink. So I told Triona I'd do it.

A few minutes later my phone rang again, this time an unrecognised number. When I answered my heart was beating hard against my ribs. It was a researcher from the radio show.

'Neil is going to read out the email after the eleven o'clock news,' he told me. 'Would you be willing to come on?'

I'd say he was shocked when I said I would. He asked me if I wanted to stay on the line until Neil was ready to speak to me. I said I would, because I knew if I hung up, I wouldn't be able to go ahead with it.

As I waited I heard Neil read out Triona's email. Halfway through it, he had to go to commercials because he got too emotional. 'When we come back, we'll have Leanne's mam on the line,' he said.

As the ads played my heart pounded. I'd never spoken in public before and my pronunciation was very poor. I found big words hard to manage. For years, because of my dyslexia, I'd pronounced things like 'guitar' as 'dictar'. I was anxious about making a laughing stock of our family.

Neil Prendeville is a very straight-up presenter. He always says what he's thinking even if it might be hard to hear. I worried that I wouldn't be able to take the hurt if he said anything negative about people who took their own lives. But there was a name behind our suicide, and it was Leanne. I wanted it known. I wanted to tell the listeners that she was my baby and I loved the bones of her.

When Neil came back on the air, he read the rest of the email. Then he said, 'I have Leanne's mother on the line.'

Just before I opened my mouth, I thought, *Please don't let this be about a heartbroken mother. Let it be about a child who lost the fight to live.*

When I began speaking to groups of people, the strangest thing happened. It was like there was no one else in the world. Everything melted away and I was just there alone, talking about my daughter. She wasn't a girl who took an overdose. She was a vibrant, living person. She had a mother and a father, she had a grandmother and aunts and uncles and cousins; she was a sister and a daughter. She loved and was loved unconditionally.

Every time I have spoken to groups of people about Leanne in the years since then, the same thing has happened. It's not like I'm talking to a crowd, it's like I'm just talking to myself.

Towards the end of the interview I became confused. 'I have three children,' I said. Then, 'No, I have two children.'

I knew I had three children, but seven weeks after Leanne's passing, I didn't know what was right. I was thinking, *What do I say now? Do people say they have only two children when once they had three?*

Neil was exceptionally kind when I voiced these thoughts out loud. 'You had three children, Collette,' he said. 'You will always have three.'

That's how the radio and television interviews began. Not a lot of people were talking about the growing problem of suicide in Ireland. Word got out that there was a woman whose daughter had taken her own life not very long ago, and she was willing to speak about it. I knew nothing about suicide, apart from my own experience, which was still so new and raw. But phone calls and requests came from radio stations and TV channels, and I felt I owed it to Leanne, to my husband and children, to talk about my daughter as a real person, not just a suicide statistic.

I'd like to say doing the radio interviews helped, that in some way it was healing to talk about Leanne's life, but the opposite is true. Every time I spoke, it was like reliving the night we lost her, and soon it began to send me over the edge altogether.

30

You might wonder why I kept saying yes to the people who called looking for interviews. To be honest, I wondered myself. I didn't want to be on the radio. I wanted to be left alone in a quiet place to lick my wounds. But with the media you're not given that chance. Calls to be on this show or that kept coming in, and some compulsion stopped me turning them down.

I know now that my need to speak was wrapped up in my guilt. I had failed Leanne, and I wanted to do whatever I could to try to make up to her. I felt that if I did the next interview, the world would know she wasn't a teenager who just threw her life away. I would be doing her some justice.

Beneath this atonement, something else was going on. Grief is a strange thing. It leads you to all sorts of thoughts that would normally be considered round the twist. After Frances was gone, I kept thinking she was still alive. After Leanne died, part of me believed she might come back. Doing the media interviews, reliving her suicide and talking about her life threw me into a kind of whirlpool at random moments: I'd see or hear something and be sucked so fully into the past, where Leanne was alive and well, that I'd forget the present.

It would feel like some sort of consolation, but when I came lurching back into the real world, where my baby was lost and gone for ever, I'd feel as if I was going insane.

I took to walking. It was the only effort I could make at trying to keep myself in one piece. I wasn't able to face going back to work and dealing with the customers and their reaction to me. I could barely face seeing anyone other than my immediate family and Mark Ryan.

But there was no refuge to be had. I'd walk past a field of cows and be sucked into the whirlpool …

Leanne is seventeen. Anthony and I have been away for the night, having left Triona in charge of Leanne and her friend, who has come to stay in our house in Rathcormac. Everything is in place and the house is spotless, except for the tiles on the kitchen floor, which feel sticky under my shoes.

I put aside my niggling suspicions that the house is *too* clean. Leanne and I are getting on brilliantly, having been through a bad patch during which she argued with me about everything, so I don't want to upset the apple cart.

Instead, I go for a walk as part of my effort to keep my weight down. Things are good. I'm working at Marks & Spencer, we've all settled into life in our new house, and I'm feeling better about my body than I have for a while.

As I walk, building up a sweat, a squad car pulls up alongside me.

'Mrs Wolfe?' says the guard driving it. He's a young man and I can see he looks a bit lost for words.

'As a garda, I have to do this,' he says apologetically. 'A complaint was made about your daughter, Leanne. She had a party in your house and she threw the evidence into a farmer's field nearby, the bottles and cans. The farmer's very upset because his cows could have choked on them.'

'Cows?' I reply, trying to get my head around the information he's given me. 'Do they eat bottles?'

The guard starts laughing. 'I've had parties in my day,' he says. 'There's no harm done, but I was just with Leanne and she's in a terrible state. She thinks you're going to kill her.'

'Kill her?' I reply. 'I'm going to hang, draw and quarter her!'

'Just bring her up to the farmer's place to apologise,' the guard says, and drives off.

I pull out my phone and call Anthony. 'Your daughter is out of control! Come home now!'

When I get home, Triona is apologetic. 'She had the whole thing planned,' she tells me. 'I couldn't stop her.'

Leanne is hiding in her room. 'I'm not angry that you had a party, I'm angry that you didn't tell me beforehand,' I say, after barging through the door. 'And what's more, you killed one of the farmer's cows! It swallowed a bottle!'

Leanne's eyebrows look like they're going to jump off her head in horror. 'Oh, Mam,' she bawls. 'I didn't mean to!'

Anthony buys a bottle of wine and a box of chocolates on the way home and we all get into the car to drive to the farmer's house.

When we get there, I tell Leanne, 'We're not going in with you.'

She bursts into tears again. 'I can't do it, Mam,' she pleads. 'Don't make me!'

'Leanne, you had your party. You have to face the consequences.'

In the end Anthony goes with her and I watch Leanne hand over the wine and chocolates at the door, still crying . . .

Suddenly the whirlpool spits me out and I'm standing on the edge of a lonely country road, staring at cows, not able to make sense of the terrible fact that Leanne is gone. A split second ago she was apologising to a farmer.

The sad thing is she wrote in her diary about killing the cow. She went to her grave thinking it was true.

'I know I'm hated, but I'm loving the attention,' one of my daughter's tormentors wrote on Bebo.

I'd log on to Leanne's page, then click through to the pages of the girls who had sent her horrible messages before she died. I wanted to know what they were doing now. I wanted to know if they were bullying anyone else. What I found was that they had no remorse, and it drove me crazy.

Anthony couldn't handle me going onto Bebo. 'You're making it worse for yourself,' he'd say. I knew I was making it worse for him, too, because I shared every word. But I couldn't stop.

I became like a private detective mounting my own investigation. Piecing together a line or two from the diary with the Bebo page and text messages on Leanne's phone, combined with a little questioning of Triona and Leanne's other friends, I found there had been an episode at the time of her eighteenth birthday. A gang of guys and girls came into the restaurant where

Leanne and her friends were celebrating – it was the night after she'd been out with her family – and started shouting at her that she was a whore.

Leanne did defend herself that night. She didn't usually, she was too afraid. But she called Triona to say, 'I'm after standing up to C. She called me all sorts of names, but I told her she was jealous because there was nobody would bother with her.'

I reckon Leanne paid a big price for that. Those girls weren't going to let it go that easily.

On St Patrick's Day, Leanne got another punch in the face. Her friend Joanne told me they were out at a club and somebody just came up and laid into Leanne. I found out other things. If she was coming out of McDonald's, for instance, heading to her car, there would always be fear. She used to say to Joanne that she was never going to get away from them. They weren't your average bullies. These people made sure on a daily basis that she had some confrontation with them.

Leanne had two phones, because she was always losing one. After the police returned them, we found hundreds of threatening texts – things like *I've seen where you parked your car and I'm going to fuck it up*. Or *We know where you'll be tomorrow night, and you're dead*.

At the end Leanne was afraid to even look at her phone. I asked Mark Ryan if she'd opened the texts that came on the night she died, and he said she had.

I was hoping she hadn't because they were horrible. I couldn't bear to think they were the last things that she saw.

I figured that, because she'd moved away from those girls and her life had become better, they were envious. That was what Triona told Leanne on St Patrick's night, after Leanne had been given a dig in the face. 'They're just jealous, girl.'

This thought gave me no relief. I walked the roads surrounding our house, fuming inside. I wanted to slaughter them. I wanted to punch and kick and bite them, to tear their hair out. I wanted them to feel every bit of pain Leanne did. I wanted to burn their houses down. I wanted to destroy their lives. I wanted their families to know the devastation I did. I wanted to run through the streets screaming about what those people had done to my daughter.

Yet when I listen back to the radio interviews I sound calm and collected. I'm grief-stricken, of course, and I talk about the bullying, but the rage that was gushing with the blood through my veins isn't noticeable.

I lived with that hidden rage for a long time, not just months but years. It took enormous changes to happen in my life, things I would never have imagined taking place, before I could learn to channel it for good.

31

I wasn't the only one in our family concealing rage.
After Anthony's outburst, when he filled his van with
tools to take his revenge, the anger seemed to go out
of him, like air from a balloon. He got on with life,
going to work and providing, but it was like the lights
were on and no one was home. He didn't express
any emotions at all. Instead he constantly made that
sound like he was trying to swallow something but it
wouldn't go down.

One night a couple of guards came to our door with
my son standing between them, looking as if he wanted
the ground to swallow him. We were shocked because

it wasn't in Ant's character to be in trouble. We'd never had a moment of worry with him in that respect. The police, too, seemed to be upset about having to knock on our door.

Ant had been driving through the city when he spotted two fellas who had been involved in bullying Leanne. He'd jumped out of his jeep, right in the middle of Patrick's Street, leaving the door open and the engine on, and went for them. Violence is against Ant's nature – he wouldn't hurt a fly – so the anger inside him must have become overwhelming. When the guards arrived on the scene, they had to literally drag him off the two guys.

Later Ant told us he'd wanted answers. How could those boys be involved in bullying a young girl? They were both nineteen years old. Why did they pick on his little sister?

The guards who brought him home to us were very kind. Some of their colleagues played football with Ant, and everyone in the station was aware of what had happened in our family. They said to us that they knew it wasn't in Ant's personality to go on the attack and they were just leaving him home for his own good. But it was awful to see my son in such turmoil. If anyone knew about wanting answers for what had happened to Leanne, it was me. I'd been searching for them, like a detective on a case, but coming up against a brick wall of pain instead.

After the incident on Patrick's Street, the father of one of the guys went to the garda station to make a complaint, saying Ant had attacked his son. But when the guards asked him why he thought that particular young man, who had no record of violence whatsoever, would abandon his vehicle in the middle of a street and do what he did, the father withdrew his complaint.

Although it was tough to see my son in such a state that night, I do remember being relieved he'd actually let something out. Since the night he'd phoned us in Lanzarote, he hadn't uttered anything about how he was feeling. He hadn't even mentioned Leanne's name. I had seen that he was pushing it all down, but I couldn't encourage him to let it up because I could barely manage my own feelings, which were all on the surface.

After the guards left, Ant became tearful. 'I'm sorry for what I did,' he said, thinking he had brought more trouble on us. Instead I was thinking that maybe this might bring him to a better place.

They say there are certain stages of grief, but I don't know if it's the same when someone you love takes their own life. Suicide leaves you with a very different grief. I know this sounds bitter, but the best way I can describe it is as a dirty grief, because there is so much guilt and confusion attached to it. As a mother, I had that dirty grief for the child I lost, but I was also constantly aware of the guilt and confusion my other children were feeling.

They were still afraid of their own shadows, too, jumping at the slightest noise, their eyes always wide in their faces. They hadn't seen this coming and they didn't know what to do with it.

When they were small, I could put all my children in one bed and get in with them, making them feel safe, secure and loved. I could give them the feeling that nothing would harm them, that our house was a safe place and our family a safe haven. But there was no getting into bed with Triona and Ant now, no giving them a sense of comfort and security. Their world had blown apart and all sense of being protected had gone.

My husband, when he at last started talking about his feelings many months later, once described our grief as a pack of black dogs. They had surrounded us, filling us with dreadful fear. That night with Ant, I could see the black dogs in his eyes. He looked bewildered, too, as if he'd woken up in the wilderness and didn't know how he'd gotten there.

Before Leanne left us, my son was forever hugging me, but now he barely came near me. Maybe he couldn't bear the thought of being comforted, the way I couldn't allow myself take anti-anxiety medication. Maybe he felt he didn't deserve it.

When they were growing up I never rooted through my children's things. I always felt they deserved their privacy, but after finding so much we should have known in Leanne's diaries, so much information that could have helped us save her, I became like a bloodhound trying to find out what was going on with Ant and Triona. I'd go through drawers in their houses, searching through bags they left down, looking for anything that might give me a hint they were thinking of taking their own lives too.

That's how I found the letter Ant wrote to Leanne. It was an apology for failing her. He said he knew she hadn't been able to come to him for help because he wasn't a fighter. Reading it made the suicide alarm ring louder in my ears. I showed it to my husband and he said I was right to be worried.

One night at about midnight, Ant's wife Debra went upstairs to check on their son Ryan. Ant was sitting in the front room watching telly, but as Debra described it afterwards, it was as if he'd disappeared inside himself. He had barely opened his mouth all day.

From Ryan's room, she heard a little thud. It was the front door closing. Ant had left the house without saying a word. After a quarter of an hour, she got a bit concerned, so she called me. Ant wasn't answering his phone.

Anthony and I got our coats on and went out looking for him around the streets, but he was nowhere to be found. At about 2 a.m., we were back sitting with Debra when I had an idea. 'Do you think he might have gone to Leanne's grave?' I said.

Anthony and I headed out to the cemetery. Driving

up to it, I saw that Ant's jeep was parked just outside the gates and my blood ran cold. We knew he was in a very dark place and we thought he would harm himself.

We jumped out of the car, and as we ran through the cemetery gates, I heard the sound of sobbing. It was pitch black. The only light we could see was the flickering of votive candles by some of the headstones.

We made our way to where Leanne was buried and found Ant stretched on her grave, crying like a baby.

His dad and I lifted him off the ground, trying to be as gentle as we could. Through his tears Ant kept repeating, 'I'm so sorry. I'm so sorry.'

I was brought back to the day we arrived home from Lanzarote and Triona saying the same thing over and over as I took her in my arms.

'It's okay, son,' I said, through my own tears. 'It's okay.'

When we got back to the gates of the cemetery, I said to Anthony, 'You take the jeep, I'll bring Ant in the car with me.' I wanted to talk to him. I knew he had something to tell.

As I drove, Ant silently cried in the passenger seat. 'What is it, son?' I asked. 'Why are you apologising? Do you think you did something wrong?'

'I can't tell you, Mam,' he said, barely able to get the words out.

I pulled into the side of the road and turned off the engine. 'You have to tell me,' I said. 'Because whatever it is, if you don't let it out, it will kill you.'

After a little bit, he began. 'You know how when her knee was sore and she couldn't drive, how she was always looking for a lift to school? She'd want you to drop her right to the door. One day I gave her a lift to the top of the hill and said she'd have to walk down because I didn't want to get caught in traffic on the way to work. She got out of the car and for a second I thought she was crying. I didn't ask her why, Mam. I let her walk down the hill by herself and drove away.'

'For the love of God, boy,' I said. 'Knowing Leanne, she would have wanted you to drive to the door and wait for her until she was finished at half past three. If that's the worst you've done to your sister, if that's what's forcing you to the end of your rope, then you have to let it go. You loved her and she loved you. I'm proud she had the brother she had in you.'

Ant shook his head slowly, not agreeing with me.

'We need to pull together to get through this,' I told him. 'Your dad and I need to know you'll be all right. Your wife needs to know you'll be all right. We all feel guilty. We all feel it was our fault. But I'm telling you now, and listen to me closely, Ant – it was not your fault. You did nothing wrong.'

It would be a long time before my son said anything about his feelings again. He didn't make a full recovery after that event, nothing near it, but at least he'd shared the nightmare he'd been left with, the black dog that was stalking him.

I was strong for him that night, I was strong as I could be for him and Triona and Anthony every day, but my own black dogs were circling and ready to pounce.

32

I almost drowned once. When you come up and go under, you barely get a gulp of air before you're engulfed again in the water. Four months after Leanne's death, I felt like I was almost constantly drowning. Every morning when I woke up, there would be a brief moment of being able to breathe before reality hit and I'd go under again. It was all grief, all loneliness, all heartache.

When we got the toxicology report on Leanne's body, we found there had been no alcohol in her blood. In fact, there was very little food in her system either. This information might have been some form of relief, given that her bullies told the police in the aftermath of her death that she'd been plastered out of her mind on vodka, but it only added to my guilt and horror. Now I imagined my child dying without anything in her stomach, starving as she lay on her bed, unable to move.

Media requests kept coming in and still I couldn't say no. Looking back, maybe I was giving the interviews to try and make sense of a death that had no sense to it at all. I agreed to be interviewed by Ciaran Cassidy for a documentary on RTÉ Radio 1 called *The Diary of Leanne Wolfe*. Anthony said he'd be part of it too.

We gave Ciaran access to the diaries, so the interview we did was intermingled with readings by a young actress playing Leanne in the final documentary.

It nearly sent us both over the edge. We'd gone through the diaries with our counsellor and, in a way, it had kept Leanne alive in our minds. We were connected to her as long as we were reading them. The documentary felt the same. We were talking about Leanne as if she was still with us, laughing at the way she'd written about driving us crazy with loud music after she'd locked herself in her room, nostalgic about her character, and it had a kind of magic about it, a way of distancing me from the truth that she was never coming back. But time was passing and we were coming more and more to confront that fact. So instead of healing, I felt emptier and emptier. The whole world felt blank, as if nothing meant anything. All that was there was the terrible, futile loss of my child.

I walked the country lanes near our house more and more. I'd look at the branches of trees and imagine hanging myself from one of them. The idea of living on in this barren, meaningless world was horrific to me.

I felt I deserved to strangle and choke with a rope around my neck, to feel awful pain as I died. How could I not have known? What kind of parents were we that we'd not been able to see our daughter was in dire distress? I felt I had failed Leanne to the extent that she'd had no choice but to take her own life. How could I live with that? How could I live in a world where this could happen? How could I live in a world where joy had been killed, replaced only by pain? How could I live with myself?

I stopped driving altogether because I knew I would close my eyes behind the wheel and I was afraid I'd kill somebody else while trying to end my own life. I was drawn to water, to the thought of jumping off a cliff. I didn't think about taking an overdose because I felt that would be too easy on me.

The only thing that held me from going any further was the thought of hurting my other two children, of leaving them in even more pain. Yet part of me felt I had been a terrible mother to them, too, that in failing Leanne I'd failed them as well. *Maybe they'd be better off without me,* I thought. Of course I knew they wouldn't be better off if their mother committed suicide, but a form of insanity had set in and these were the thoughts constantly running through my mind, every empty day and sleepless night. It was never-ending.

The hardest thing to battle with was that I never got to hold her. Every mother would want to hold their child as they were going out of the world, telling them it will be okay. I wasn't there to comfort her as the life left her body. She'd been absolutely alone.

The only solace came when Mark Ryan called to our door. From the night he'd sat and said his prayer for us, he'd shared more and more stories about God and the church he and his family went to. I still didn't believe in any God, but more than that, I didn't believe I deserved any God's love. Yet I felt that Mark connected to what I was feeling more than anyone else could. On those nights when he sat at our kitchen table, I felt less hollow. I'm not saying he took away my grief, but he brought a tiny bit of peace.

In a way, I was fascinated with him too. It was so strange to see a guard in full uniform, standing in the middle of my kitchen, praying for me. He provided a distraction from the daily grind of my grief.

On the outside, I looked like I was coping, being strong for my children, getting through the day-to-day things. But I was barely hanging on. One morning I was staring at the patio door with the idea of running straight through it and not stopping. But where was there to run to? Nowhere.

I had never been so alone in my life. I believed I had nothing to live for.

I phoned our counsellor and said, 'Eleanor, is this my life?'

She said, 'It is, Colette, but you have to learn to work around it.'

I hung up, thinking, *She has no idea of what I've worked around in my life. How could anyone work around this?*

I phoned Anthony at work and said, 'Is this my life?'

'It is,' he replied. 'We have to suck it up.'

It sounded wrong and too like what Eleanor had said, so I hung up on him as well.

I phoned Triona, and by the time she answered, I was crying so hard, I couldn't get any words out. I'd been trying for five months to hold myself together in front of her and Ant, but now I'd lost all my powers of control.

'Mam,' Triona said. 'You have to calm down.' I could hear fear in her voice.

I did my best to catch my breath and talk. I told her I was feeling very low, but I didn't say what I was really thinking, that I wanted to die.

Maybe she could hear the truth between my words. 'You should go to that church Mark Ryan talks about,' she said.

I thought, *This girl must really be at the end of her rope with me, if she's telling me to go to church.* But another notion crept up: *I've lost everything as it is, so what do I have to lose?*

After Triona hung up, I phoned Anthony again. 'We're going to church,' I told him. He didn't put up any fight.

Then I called Mark Ryan.

'Where's that church you're always going on about?' I asked him.

He was very calm, as if he'd been expecting my call. He told me where it was and that the next service was in two days' time.

'I don't want anyone coming near us,' I warned him. 'We're very vulnerable. If anybody starts trying to save our mortal souls, we won't be staying.'

'Don't worry, Collette,' he said. 'It's not that kind of place.'

33

My sister Rosarie had to dress me for church because I was so nervous. She fed me little bits of orange to build my energy up because I was hardly eating at all. Having learned that Leanne's stomach was empty when she died, I couldn't allow myself much in the way of food. I felt I deserved to go hungry because Leanne had starved on her deathbed.

It didn't look like an ordinary church. Instead of an altar there was a raised area at the top of the room, like a stage, with a screen on the wall behind it. There were no statues or confessionals, no stations of the cross. In the rows of plastic chairs there were all kinds of people of every nationality. Anthony and I sat down at the back, keeping ourselves to ourselves.

A group of women and men, all wearing purple gowns, like the kind you see in films with graduation days, walked onto the stage. They began singing a song and the lyrics came up on the screen behind them. They weren't words about sin or punishment or dying on a cross: they were about love.

People got up to dance in the aisles. They lifted their hands towards the ceiling and sang along. In the back row, Anthony and I sat watching, open-mouthed, trying to take it all in. When Mark talked in our kitchen about going to church, this was the last thing I'd imagined. I'd been visualising the cold cathedrals I'd kneeled in as a child, those places where I'd not been allowed to make any noise as an old priest droned on and on about things I didn't understand.

This place was all noise. It was full of colour and joy. The message couldn't have been simpler: *God loves you.*

A man got up after the choir had finished and spoke about God's love. Rather than a priest, he was called a pastor. Then he asked people to come up and tell their stories. People queued, and when they got to the stage, they talked about terrible things that had happened in their lives, or the trials they were going through at the moment. They were all smiling. Some of them laughed out loud through tears. They all talked about how grateful they were that God was here to love them.

I looked at their happiness as they talked about their pain, and I thought, *Whatever these people believe in, it's very real to them.* A part of me felt jealous. I wanted that belief. I wanted the comfort it seemed to give.

My eyes met Anthony's and we were both crying. I wasn't sure why the tears poured down my cheeks. We didn't get up to dance, but we stayed until the end of the service. It had been a long time since I'd had a moment of feeling safe, but that night in that place, I gained a bit of safety. I didn't really understand the reason why, but I didn't want to question. There was such relief in it.

We went back the following Sunday, and again and again after that. I didn't believe in the God that everyone was so joyful about, but I liked sitting there. Every day was a struggle to live, but for a few hours at church I could just be without thinking. I could listen to people sharing about their lives, and most of all, I could listen to the stories the pastor told. They brought me back to a happy part of my childhood, something I'd completely forgotten.

I must have been about ten years of age when the film *The Ten Commandments* came to the Capitol cinema in Cork. All the girls in my school were taken by the nuns to see it.

I loved every minute of the almost four hours it

took to tell the whole story. I'd never even heard the Ten Commandments described like this before, or of Moses, who was played by Charlton Heston. He was like God, this big, muscly man with a beard; he was wise and kind and strong. He carried a staff and he used it to part the sea so the thousands of slaves following him could walk to safety.

The slaves' enemies were in hot pursuit and my heart was in my mouth because I was sure they were going to catch them. But then Moses brought the water down on top of the bad guys and the slaves made it to the Promised Land. It was a beautiful place, where nothing could harm them.

All my own worries seemed to depart as I sat there, transfixed. I brought them to school with me, I brought them home, I brought them everywhere, but in the Capitol cinema that day they were banished like Moses' enemies. My guard was totally down. I was a child who never, ever let her guard down, so watching *The Ten Commandments* felt like respite.

Going to church gave me the same kind of feeling. The pastor's stories were like movies I could get lost in. God wasn't real for me. He was just part of a good yarn that took my mind away from the pain. He couldn't be real unless He stood there in front of me and said, 'Hello, Collette, I'm God.' And I knew that wasn't going to happen.

But then something *did* happen. We'd been going

to church regularly for a few months by the time the pastor told the story of King David bringing the Ark of the Covenant to Jerusalem. I didn't understand at first what the ark was, but the pastor explained that it was actually God's presence with us.

There were all sorts of celebration going on, music and dancing, and when King David got to the gates of Jerusalem with the ark, he stripped off and started dancing in the streets too.

As the pastor told the story, I thought, *I never heard of anything like this in the Bible.* In fact, I'd never even opened a Bible. Every time I saw one in a hotel room, I'd shut the drawer on it.

All sorts of images were appearing in my head. The people dancing and celebrating, the colour and noise, the praising of God, the sacrificing of the fatted calf …

King David's wife, Michal, was watching all the celebrations from the window of their house and she was disgusted with her husband for stripping off and dancing, like a commoner, with the slave girls. When he came home, she had a go at him, telling him he'd made a complete fool of himself and his family.

But he stopped her in her tracks and said, 'I'm singing and praising the king who gave me this kingdom, and I'm going to always praise him because I am a lucky man.'

From the pulpit, the pastor asked, 'Who are you?

Are you the person at the window looking down, or are you David, dancing?'

Time stood still and I felt he was talking directly to me. I'd been a person looking out the window all my life, afraid to join in with anything, afraid that people would know who I really was – a dirty woman, who didn't deserve to be loved.

Don't let anyone get too close. Don't get too close to anyone, because you'll get hurt. That was the motto I'd lived by, and look where it had brought me.

'If you want to be David, dancing, put up your hand,' the pastor said. I don't know how, but my hand raised itself of its own accord.

It's hard to describe the feeling that was happening inside me. I was overcome with emotion, thinking of myself alone and looking out that window. I wanted more than anything to be dancing. I can't say why, but in that moment I knew for a fact that God wasn't just a figment of the imagination. He was real.

The pastor asked if we wanted to say a prayer, to acknowledge that God was here, and to ask Him into our lives. I sobbed through the whole prayer, my body shaking. It wasn't like crying with grief and pain, it was a different kind of crying. It wasn't happiness either. The nearest way I can describe it is as an overwhelming sense of liberation.

What I didn't realise was that when the pastor asked who wanted to dance like David, Anthony had raised his hand at exactly the same time as I did. He said the prayer too, asking God into his life.

That day, we both came to believe in God. But one of us felt they deserved God's love more than the other, and this would become the straw that broke the camel's back.

34

From the time I was eight years old, I always felt unclean. Even when, as a grown woman, I had sex with my husband there was always a voice in the back of my head telling me that what I was doing was dirty and as a result I was dirty too.

At church I discovered that God existed, so I didn't have to search for Him any more. But for me at that time, He wasn't the loving God that everyone there talked about. I thought there was no way He could want anything to do with me. Why would this God, who was good and kind and wonderful, want someone dirty like me? Why would he want someone who had done nothing right in her life?

Motherhood was the one thing I'd thought I'd gotten right, but Leanne's death proved I'd failed at that too. I couldn't get away from this fact. God couldn't lift the burden of guilt from me, and He couldn't love me because of it.

Anthony, on the other hand, took to God like a duck to water. Mark Ryan gave us a gift of a beautiful Bible, which he read every night. Then he got a smaller version, which he could bring to work with him. Every moment he got, he'd have his nose in a Bible. Within weeks I saw a change in him. The gaunt look was lifting, along with the terror in his eyes. It was like he had this peaceful aura growing around him.

I wish I could say that I was happy for him that he was finding comfort, but I wasn't. Inside I battled against it mightily. He was going to have peace while I'd be left in suffering. More than anything I was afraid that I was losing him now too. It was like he was becoming sealed off in a place I didn't have access to.

I knew he was trying to hide it from me. It was like a little secret he had between himself and God, and I wasn't in on it.

A little bit of me thought that maybe men handled it differently. Maybe Anthony was able to move on without Leanne, while I, her mother, would never do it. Yet another part of me knew what a good father he was. I remembered his screams that night in Lanzarote and I just couldn't understand how he seemed to be coming to terms with the loss of Leanne.

Sometimes I asked him to read to me from the Bible, which he did willingly. I was searching for relief more than belief. I wanted the stories and the psalms to transport me the way I was taken out of my misery when I went to church. After a while it became a routine with us, Anthony reading pages of the Bible in the evenings while I listened in silence, asking a question here and there about what he thought it meant. I did it to share in this new world with him, even though I didn't think I was worthy of it.

I went further and further into isolation. The counselling wasn't working for me any more. I kept going to church, and that continued to provide some kind of respite, but I was constantly reminded of being not good enough for God's love.

Triona's daughter, Hollie, was born on 5 December 2007. I held her and felt nothing. All I thought was that Leanne would never hold her own baby. I would never see her have children, never see her get married, never see her graduate. I looked at the innocent little infant in my arms and thought, *How could I be of any use to you? I'm an appalling mother, so I couldn't possibly be a good grandmother*.

By the time Hollie came into the world we were

facing Leanne's inquest, which was scheduled to take place a week later, on 12 December. When we got the date, Mark Ryan sat Anthony and me down and talked us through what would probably take place. But there was no real way to prepare us for it. We certainly weren't prepared to learn that three of the young people Leanne named in her diaries were subpoenaed to be at the inquest. Although I wanted answers about what had finally pushed my daughter to take an overdose, I was distraught when I heard those people would be present. The thought of seeing them revolted me. I'd read the texts that had been sent to my daughter the night she died and the messages on her Bebo page, and the idea that these people might say terrible things about Leanne in a court of law filled me with dread. I didn't know how I'd be able to sit there and take it.

Although an inquest takes place in a courtroom, it's not a trial. Nobody goes under oath. There's no arguing back and forth between barristers, no witnesses for or against any accused, no conviction for a crime. It's simply an inquiry into the cause of a sudden, unexplained or violent death. The fact that those teenagers had been subpoenaed confused me, though. As Anthony, Ant, Triona and I all drove to Cobh for the inquest, I felt as if we were going to a trial. I had a vain hope that some justice might come from it.

I brought the diaries with me. I felt that they represented her voice because she couldn't speak for herself. When we got into the court and sat down, I could feel the tension in my husband, son and daughter, like there were electric currents coming from them. It looked as if they might just lose control of their emotions at any second. I told myself, as I had the night Leanne died and the days before her funeral, that I had to be the one to stay grounded. I wanted to hear every word that was said in that courtroom.

The coroner came out and Leanne's case was called. The pathologist who had done Leanne's post-mortem came up, Dr Margaret Bolster. She was a very professional woman, and a kind woman, I'd say, but it was harrowing to hear her refer to Leanne as 'the body'. I was thinking, *She's not a body. She was my baby. I pushed her into the world.*

It was all very cold and clinical, a detailed examination of every part of Leanne's body. Dr Bolster listed the weight of her organs, her heart and lungs, and I wondered how they'd be able to do that unless they'd removed them. Then a picture of my child's heart being taken out came into my mind.

Beside me, Triona and Anthony were sobbing. My son was pale as a ghost – he looked like he wanted to disappear. The pathologist talked about what bruises Leanne had, the scar on her knee from getting her cruciate ligament removed. It even came down to the fact that she was wearing panties. Leanne was such a private person, she'd kept so many secrets, and here was her whole body being talked about in front of everyone. I remember thinking she would probably have died with embarrassment if she'd been there.

As was written in the toxicology report, the pathologist confirmed that Leanne had died of an overdose of paracetamol and codeine. We learned that she had died slowly, that her organs shut down one by one. I wondered had she lain there hoping someone would find her. I thought about how frightened she must have been.

Dr Bolster added that no alcohol had been detected in her system at the time of her death.

Then the people subpoenaed to appear were called up to give their account of what happened. They said they'd met up with Leanne on the night she'd taken the overdose and that they'd all gone drinking after purchasing vodka at an off-licence in Blackpool. They said she had been in 'high spirits' and had been laughing and joking with them.

I sat there thinking, *How can they tell such barefaced lies? Hasn't the pathologist just said there was no alcohol in her system?*

The coroner called the pathologist up again and she was asked to explain the toxicology report once more. She repeated that there had been nothing in Leanne's system, no food or alcohol, so there was no way she could have been drinking that night.

The teenagers were called to the stand again. They stuck to their story about Leanne drinking litres of vodka.

That night, Leanne had got home at about 2 a.m. Triona heard her come up the stairs. She opened the door to Triona's bedroom and the hall light shone in, waking her up. Triona said, 'Are you all right, girl?' and Leanne replied, 'I am, Triona.'

Triona asked her if she wanted to come and get into her bed.

'No,' Leanne said. 'I'll sleep in my own room.'

'Did you have a nice night?' Triona asked, and Leanne said it had been grand. Then she said, 'Night, Triona. I love you.'

Those were her last words. When Triona returned from work late the following evening, she looked in on Leanne and found her in a deep sleep in her room. Figuring she was still tired from being out the night before, she left her alone. She didn't know then that Leanne had never left her room from the previous night.

Something must have happened that night to push her over the edge. Mark Ryan reckoned that some altercation had taken place earlier in the evening, but no matter how many questions were asked by the police, nobody has ever said anything about it. There's nothing written in Leanne's diary, but the text she got on her phone after she came home points to some sort of confrontation.

You, you whore, on my nan's soul you wouldn't want to bump into me anytime soon, I swear, because I'm going to break your face. You're worse than the prostitutes.

In her diaries, Leanne wrote that name-calling was worse than the beatings. She must have been thinking, *I can never fix it now. It's over for me.*

One day somebody won't be able to hold on to the secret. Whatever happened that night will come out and we'll get another bit of the jigsaw puzzle. In the meantime, I only have my imagination to fill in the gaps.

When I was called to the stand, I pushed my outrage down, thinking, *I only have this chance to speak up for my daughter.*

I told the coroner that I was Leanne's voice and that I owed it to my daughter to get the message out about the dangers of bullying.

'A car crash is bad but suicide is hard to take,' I told him. 'On the morning of her burial, we found her diaries and they completely overwhelmed us. We found out about the ongoing bullying by a group of six – two more than others. Leanne had put up with a lot of physical and verbal abuse.

'The Leanne we knew wasn't the Leanne in the diaries. I wouldn't recognise the child in the diaries.

It is very obvious she took her own life because of physical and verbal abuse.

'I am ashamed to say that I am her mother and I did not know that side of her life.'

In his summation, the coroner said he could not explore why Leanne had taken her life. But he said it was important to draw attention to the question of bullying. He said there was no suggestion that the teenagers who had given evidence at the inquest had been in any way involved in bullying Leanne.

A verdict of death by self-cause was recorded, and then it was all over. I sat there stunned, thinking, *It's been proven that they lied about Leanne drinking. Why isn't something being done?*

Outside the courthouse there were reporters everywhere, all looking for comments. The teenagers scurried away with their heads down. I knew that a moment had come to speak on behalf of Leanne, and on behalf of all people who are bullied.

'My daughter would not have taken her own life if she hadn't been bullied,' I said to the assembled press. 'Victims of bullying need to confide in their loved ones. Leanne isn't the only person. There are thousands like her out there.'

When I got home, I felt chilled to my bones. My husband and children looked perished too. I didn't want to talk to anyone, so I went to my room and shut the door.

All I could think about was how long it took her to die, about how lonely she must have been, about how it might have been a cry for help and that she wanted to be saved.

I thought about the weight of her heart and lungs. After that, things started going rapidly downhill for me. I started using alcohol, more to get me to sleep than to numb the pain. I felt I deserved my pain, but at night it became unmanageable. I'd lie wide awake beside Anthony and think about my own death. The drinking got out of control very quickly, going from one bottle of wine a night to two, three, four. I poured glasses for Anthony too, and he drank with me. I think I was using it to hold on to him, to keep him from leaving me for God.

Christmas came and things got worse. All through the children's growing up, Anthony and I had had different attitudes to Christmas. He figured it was far too commercial, that it should be simple and about family. I was one of those people who went crazy buying presents. I loved seeing the surprise on my children's faces when I bought them extravagant things.

Have you ever noticed that there's a kind of hush on Christmas Eve? A quiet kind of expectation, as if everyone in the world is waiting for Santa. I always worked on the morning of Christmas Eve, and I felt that even in Marks & Spencer there was that hushed anticipation. In the afternoon I'd clean the house from top to bottom.

Anthony would take the three children to town, and when they got back, the place would be sparkling. There wouldn't even be a sock in the wash basket.

Every year, Leanne persuaded me to hand over a present on Christmas Eve rather than wait for the next morning, when everyone else exchanged gifts.

'Mam, give me one of my presents,' she'd beg.

'No, Leanne, I won't. Every year I do it, and then you phone Triona, telling her you've got your present already, and then she calls me, saying it's not fair.'

'But, Mam, please! I'm dying to see what you got me. I won't say anything to Triona, I promise!'

So I'd relent and take one of the parcels from under the tree for her, and next thing she'd be squealing with delight as she unwrapped it, forgetting her promise and running off to phone her sister.

That first Christmas Eve without Leanne, there wasn't the slightest echo of her delight from years gone by. There was still a hush, but it wasn't filled with expectation. It wasn't filled with anything at all. There was nothing but loneliness.

I got through it like the walking dead. I bought presents for my husband, for Triona and Ant and their children, and they gave me presents in return, but I could hardly be in the same room as them. All the Christmas songs in the shops sounded horrific to my ears, all the pictures of delighted children and laughing parents made me want to crawl under a rock and never come out again.

The only thing that held me upright was that we could go to church on Christmas Day. For the first while I'd kept the fact that we were going from my family, but gradually I'd told them.

My mother was surprised, not because it wasn't a Catholic church but because of the reaction I always had when she'd brought up religion in the past. When I had troubles, she'd say, 'Bring it to God,' and I'd go mad at her because I thought it was all a load of nonsense.

From the moment I told her I was going to a Christian church, she was dying to get her feet in there to see what it was like. She was nosy like that, always wanting to know what was going on. She'd never been in a Christian church, and she confused it with the Jehovah's Witnesses.

'What are the Jehovahs doing now?' she'd ask, and I'd think she was making fun of it a bit. But one day she said to me, 'Don't stop going to that church, Collette. I think it's helping you.'

She vowed to come to the Christmas service, and I was dying for her to come, but on the day itself she was sick. My sisters Rosarie and Loretta came, as did my niece Jessica and Frances's son, Clifford. It was just a short service, with all singing, and just like Anthony and I had on the very first day we went to church, all my family ended up crying.

After Christmas passed, the days stretched out into

more emptiness and I spiralled down even further into depression. I felt like I was barely drawing breath.

I'd been out of work for a year after Leanne, and one day soon after my return, I was in a dark place, unable to do much of anything. I'd been put on menswear for some reason, maybe because they were shifting me around the place to try and manage my inability to do any actual work. A woman came in and told me her daughter was getting married. She wanted to buy suits for her sons.

I asked her how many there were and she said, 'Five.' Then she stopped. 'Well, I had six,' she went on, 'but my youngest son is gone. He died from bone cancer two years ago after a long fight.'

I said I was sorry to hear it, and inside I became desperate to get away from her. I was worried that she might ask me if I had children, and how many there were. I didn't want to tell her about Leanne. Her son had fought to live; my daughter had taken her own life.

'Do you have children yourself?' the woman asked.

I contemplated lying and saying no, but I couldn't bring myself to deny my family, so I said, 'Yes, I do.'

'Oh, lovely. How many do you have?'

'I had three, but now I have two.'

I was praying she wouldn't ask me how my daughter had died, but she did.

'She took her life,' I said, and shame welled up in me like a sickening fog.

I will never forget this woman's words. She put her arms around me and said, 'I'm so sorry for you. I got a beautiful year with my son to say goodbye. You got nothing.'

I was amazed. I had thought she might say, 'Your daughter threw her life away. What a waste.' But instead she had compassion for what I was going through.

The pitiful thing is that I thought I didn't deserve her kindness. I let her hug me, I heard her words, but my heart couldn't take them in.

I had to let someone else take care of her and go home. I sat alone in my kitchen thinking, *There are lovely people in the world, but that doesn't change anything.*

That night as I lay in bed, I thought about waking up the next morning, about having to make it through another day, and I knew the end had come. I couldn't do it any more.

The next morning, I said to Anthony, 'I'll drive myself to work today.'

'I'll drive you in, Collette. There's no problem,' he said.

I picked up the car keys. 'No, Anthony, I'm all right to do it.'

I could see the reluctance in his eyes as he kissed my cheek. I kissed him back and told him goodbye.

Instead of going to work, I pulled into Cork railway station. I wanted the biggest, fastest train to hit me and put me out of my pain. I needed it to stop. I wanted the emptiness that death would bring, because it couldn't be worse than the big empty void that was inside me.

Part of me wanted to be with Leanne. It wasn't the idea of being in the afterlife with her. Her body was in the ground and I wanted to lie there, too, beside her. She was gone, but somehow I thought her pain was going on and on, like my own. If I died, it could all stop. I wanted to find a way to tell my beautiful daughter that I was sorry I didn't protect her.

In my mind's eye I could see Anthony handing her to me the day she was born. I could remember the joy I'd felt because I knew she was mine. I saw her take her first steps, heard her say her first words. But all those memories had been torn into shreds. Now all I could see was her swollen face in a coffin, and that coffin going into the ground.

There's a Cork saying, 'Pull up your drawers and get on with it.' I'd done that all my life and I felt I just couldn't any more. I wanted my baby back, but I couldn't get her back, so I was going to see could I go to her.

Death was the only place where I would find freedom from pain, from loneliness, from shame, from guilt. I picked up a bit of paper from the floor of the car to scribble a suicide note. But how could I leave a note when I couldn't even spell? Then I thought I'd just write 'Sorry' because I could spell that.

Anthony, Triona and Ant would be heartbroken, and my grandchildren Adam, Ryan and Hollie would have this legacy, but the urge to get out of the car was so strong. I knew if I got out, I would never be getting back in again.

A howling began to come out of me, like the wails of a starving infant. Then I found myself shouting. I was roaring at God.

'If you're really there, help me! Help me!'

I felt a kind of warmth rising in the car. A thought came into my head and somehow it wasn't my own.

When people say, 'God spoke to me,' you might imagine that a heavenly voice came out of nowhere and said the words they needed to hear. For me, the voice of God appeared like a light bulb going on in my head.

'There are two badges,' He said. 'You can choose which one you want. One is that you can get out of the car and end it here. But if you take the other badge, I will carry you.'

I could feel Him, that wonderful warmth all around me, and I knew in my heart and soul that I was going to be okay. I was going to be held and helped. The feeling of love in me was like nothing I'd ever known before, and my heart filled with hope.

I cried out, 'I'll take that badge! I'll take that badge!'

I stumbled out of the car and dialled Anthony's number. I was crying and laughing at the same time and I said to him over and over again, 'Jesus loves me, Anthony! He loves me!'

I could hear him weeping at the other end of the line. 'I know, Collette,' he said. 'I know.'

Anthony hadn't known I was planning to throw myself under a train, but he knew I wasn't coming home when I walked out the door that morning.

Instead of killing myself, I went to work. It was like I floated through the doors of Marks & Spencer. I'd never felt anything like that before. I glided over to the children's department, where we were taking a nightwear delivery, and set about my duties.

A few minutes later, another thought popped into my mind. I had heard a voice in my head. Maybe I was schizophrenic.

A wave of dread washed over me. I was suddenly sure I was going to be locked away because I was mad, so instead of ending my life, now I'd have to deal with schizophrenia. I worked myself into such a state that I ended up lying on the floor in a full-on panic attack, holding my throat. I couldn't breathe.

A manager came running over. He was a young man and he wasn't equipped for this. He dashed off to get someone else and came back with a woman I'd worked with for years.

Through my panic, I could hear her voice in my ear. It was very gentle and calm. 'Collette, what is it? What's wrong?'

I began to calm down, and after a while she got me sitting up, encouraging me to breathe slowly.

'What brought this on?' my colleague asked.

There was no way I was going to tell her, because I thought I'd be put in a straitjacket and carted off.

But her eyes were so kind and encouraging. 'God spoke to me,' I whispered, looking around in case there was anyone else to hear me. 'I was going to kill myself this morning and then His voice was in my head. He said He'd carry me.'

'Oh, Collette.' She smiled. 'He's come to heal you. I knew He would.'

I gaped at her. 'How did you know?' I asked.

'I'm a Christian,' she said.

I couldn't believe my ears. All the time we'd worked together I never knew she was a Christian. 'You Christians seem to pop up everywhere!' I said.

Afterwards, I learned from the Bible that when God shows Himself, he will always find a way to confirm it. I knew that this woman was there to confirm that what had happened to me in my car was real.

I couldn't know it that morning, but when I'd made the choice not to end my own life, I'd chosen a path that I'd never have imagined for myself. To begin with it felt like my own precious secret – *God is real and He loves me*. I was going to do my very best to learn everything I could about this God whom I'd never actually done anything for, but who had told me He'd care for me. I was going to learn how to love Him in return.

There's an old saying, 'To the world you're one person, but to me you're the world.' I understood that God felt this way about me. I'd been brought back from the brink of death. I'd been saved. All God asked in return was that I get to know Him.

In all the stories about people who find God and are

saved, that's the end. They walk off into the sunset, hand in hand with the Lord, and live happily ever after. My journey, however, had not ended. I had found a path towards making peace with Leanne's death. God had told me I would be carried on that path. But nothing comes so simply. There is always a price to be paid.

36

A letter from my mam, written to me just after Christmas 2008, four months before she passed away

Where to start …
Collette, you asked me time and time again if this is your life. I don't know if I ever helped. All I can say is if I went anywhere, I always felt I'd left something behind. I know now it was always a part of me. A part of me went with Frances and Annabelle, but life has to go on.

You and Anthony had a good life. Try to do more holidays. You had come to that time in your lives. Don't stop, it's still that time of your lives.

Try to be happy. Don't forget that life is to be enjoyed. Keep on your walks …

When Rosarie and I were leaving the hospital, the doctor gave us a book about how to look after a family member who is terminal. I asked Rosarie to buy four scratch cards and give them to you a month after I go to the happy hunting ground.

I got frightened when the doctor told us. I did not know where I was going. The one thing I knew is that Leanne and Leazelle were in my dreams every night, telling me I'm going to be fine. I think they are coming for me.

Leanne told me in a dream that I just have to wait for a while. I think it was a dream, love. I don't know any more because my head gets so fussed.

I am very tired, love, and I know there is not a lot of time left. Be happy. Know that I will be in your dreams. I love you. Hope you win on the scratch cards.

Mam

My mother cheated death so many times – she was like Lazarus in the Bible. But just over a year after Leanne left us, my mam finally passed away from bowel cancer.

She was sick for four months before she went, and they were very hard months. We promised her she would stay in her own house to the end, so between Rosarie, Loretta and me, we all took our turns staying with her, with nurses from Marymount coming in at regular times to tend her and give her the medication she needed. I did the night shifts. Anthony would collect me at seven thirty every morning, I'd do my shift at Marks & Spencer, then sleep in the afternoon and go back to my mam's in the evening.

In the last few weeks, she slipped into a kind of coma. They'd stopped feeding her, except for the medication drips in her arm.

One night I was sitting with her. Downstairs, the house was full of people, but there were just the two of us in the bedroom. She was as still as a statue, her chest barely rising and falling with her breath. It hadn't been a year since I'd buried my daughter; I wasn't ready for another funeral. I wasn't prepared to lose her.

I got onto the bed and lay down beside her, telling her I didn't want her to leave me. From the depths of her coma, my mam put her hand out and rubbed my head. It was only for a couple of seconds, but the comfort I got from it was immense. I knew the hand of God was moving hers to console me.

As sometimes happens, she rallied for a few days before she died, coming out of her unconsciousness. She laughed and joked with us, and it was like she was back for good. When we were alone together, she told me she'd been talking to Leanne, telling her she wasn't ready to go just yet.

'Where is she, Mam?' I asked, but she wasn't able to answer.

She slipped away again, her loss of consciousness

helped by the morphine she was being given for her pain. All four of us, Loretta, Rosarie, Jessica and myself, were there one night. The nurses had warned us not to give her a drink, that she was getting her liquids intravenously, but Loretta felt sorry for her because her lips were all chapped and dry. She let a drop of water into her mouth and suddenly my mam started choking so hard, you'd have heard the noise three streets away.

I got such a shock that I legged it out of the room. There I was, the daughter who had promised I wouldn't leave her side, running from the place!

The doctor came, with the Marymount nurses, and they settled her. My sisters and I laughed afterwards, because Mam would have loved the story of us all doing a runner. She had a great sense of humour.

Before she got very sick, I asked her, 'If you die before me, will you give me a sign that Leanne is all right?'

'I'll come back as a bird,' she said, dead serious.

'I don't want no bird,' I said.

'What about a breeze?' she asked.

I wanted to choke her! 'You're reading too many magazines,' I said. 'Get a grip!'

She went quiet for a moment, then said, 'You will know, Collette, I promise.'

I wasn't by Frances's side when she died, and it was always something I regretted. I didn't see my father die, or my sister Annabelle. Leanne died alone without anyone to comfort her. So, with my mam, I had this obsession that I wanted to be with her at the end. I wanted to see death. I wanted to face this thing that had taken my baby.

As it turned out, we were all there, her children and grandchildren. She had a very high complexion, a scarlet red, and all of a sudden her skin went chalk-white. It was as if the colour had been sucked out of her. I thought, *My God almighty, that's death.* It was awful to see, and there was no sense of an afterlife to it, just a final ending.

But it wasn't the end. Her eyes flipped open, she looked up, and it was as if she could see something. Then her hands lifted towards the ceiling. And then the strangest thing happened. The whole room broke out singing.

The song was 'When You Wore A Tulip (And I Wore A Big Red Rose)'. It was her party piece. She was known for singing it about my dad, although it was far from tulips he would have been giving her.

There had been no prior decision to sing it, no mention of it at all. It was like joy had broken out in the room. I remember feeling confusion. It wasn't meant to be like this. I was meant to be tearing the hair out of my head, but there I was singing. What we were really doing was telling her, 'We know you're going, Annie, but we're letting you know that we're all here with you.'

At the moment her final breath left her body, Anthony's phone started ringing. He took it out to silence the call, then leaned over to show me the display.

'Look, Collette,' he whispered. 'It's seven o'clock.'

Seven was Leanne's favourite number. Her car had four sevens in the registration. Every morning after she went to school, I'd find Boots No7 foundation left on the table. After she died, we had grass seed laid in the back garden. When it grew, there was a big number seven in the middle of it, made of different-coloured grass.

My mam didn't come back as a bird or a breeze. She'd been dying for weeks and could have gone at any moment, but she went at exactly 7 p.m. I took it as her sign to me that she was with Leanne.

On the day before Leanne took the overdose, she went to see my mam. She'd brought her usual takeaway with her, a three-in-one chips, curry and rice. Mam had the place cleaned up because it was one of the younger grandchildren's birthdays and she was giving a party. Leanne just plonked down with her takeaway, throwing the chipper paper on the kitchen table, not caring that it was all laid out for the party. My mam didn't chastise her: she had a real soft spot for Leanne.

Leanne chatted and laughed as she ate her chips that day, and it seemed like one of her ordinary visits.

Mam was bewildered by Leanne's suicide. She'd been through the deaths of two daughters and two other grandchildren, and in the middle of her grief she'd always seemed strong and able to cope. She came from a generation where they just had to get up and get on with it, no matter what went on in life. But Leanne's death floored her. She didn't say much, but you could see in her eyes that she just couldn't come to terms with it.

When she died, I knew she was at peace. She looked as if she was resting. One of the nurses from Marymount came into the room.

'Can I ask you something?' I said to her.

'You can, Collette.'

'In your job do you experience good and evil?'

'Sometimes when a family member dies, we'll know that there was difficulty in the background. People rarely say anything, but there's an atmosphere you can pick up on, a presence in the room. It's all sadness and no joy. And then you see the opposite. There's sadness, but joy too. There's a presence of love. Like with your mother. I've never seen that before, where everyone sang. It was like you were singing your mam into God's hands.'

I wondered what had been present when Leanne died. Did she feel any love in the room? I thought about Frances's morning coat wrapped around her, and how Frances had adored my daughter. Her own sister, Triona, loved her, and she was just next door. Her brother loved her, and he was just down the road.

Anthony and I loved her and our presence was in the house, even if we weren't physically there.

I couldn't sing Leanne into God's hands, but I wished that some presence of love had been with her that night.

As the nurse told me about the people she'd attended out of this life, I hoped that Leanne had felt God's love. It was the first moment I'd felt hope since she died.

37

Nowadays when I speak in the media about Leanne's death, I talk about being at peace with it. This is a message of hope for some, but others just can't understand it. Some are cynical: they say I must be making it up. Others get angry. They rail against the idea of recovering from the loss of a child or coming to terms with suicide. I understand why they might. If some woman had turned up on the air in the weeks after Leanne died and told me there was peace to be found after your child had taken their own life, I would have thrown the radio out the window. I would have screamed at her, even though she couldn't hear me, that I didn't deserve peace, that the idea of being at peace would have been an insult to my child's memory, that there was nothing but pain to be had from this.

The peace I have experienced is not about forgetting. It's not about painlessness. The loss of a child is always part of who you are and won't go away, and you never come to terms with the thoughts of your child taking their own life. But in the midst of all the pain and heartache, the confusion, guilt and shame that Leanne's death brought into my life, I was able to find peace at the core of my being. The beginning of that peace first made itself known on the day in my car when God spoke to me. It was like a little seed had been planted inside, ready to sprout and grow. It just needed the right conditions to help it along. For me, that meant going to church, reading the Bible and praying.

Now that I knew God was with me, I prayed to Him to take my pain away. More than that, I prayed for there to be some meaning to my pain. Otherwise what was it all for? I still wanted some kind of answer for Leanne's death.

What I've learned in the months and years since then is that God's answers rarely come directly. Sometimes it's not the answer you want, but you find out later on that it's the right one. He has a way of making them known on the inside, rather than showing you on the outside. Indeed, He's often answered already, even before you've asked the question. The answer I needed was contained in the interviews I'd been doing about Leanne. I couldn't at the time say what my compulsion was for speaking to the media, but now I know that I was being guided towards meaning.

Anthony and I were asked to go on TV3's *Ireland AM*. Suicide among young people had become a subject the whole country was talking about, and the producers wanted us to share Leanne's story. After the emotional fallout from doing the RTÉ Radio 1 documentary about her diaries, I was reluctant, but a more powerful force was driving me on and I felt I couldn't say no. Anthony was even more reticent than me, but I couldn't do it without him at my side. He wouldn't say much, I knew, but he was like a rock I could lean on in front of the cameras.

Because we had to be at the studio at the crack of dawn, we drove to Dublin the night before and stayed in a hotel. We were so wound up about going on television, neither of us slept a wink. I'd had my hair blow-dried the day before and had my own make-up with me. That's what I grew up with: you put your face on before you faced the world. Leanne was like that too.

That morning I did my make-up in the hotel room like an expert, but my heart was almost jumping out of my chest. I was an ordinary, uneducated woman about to go on live TV. The pressure to be able to speak without making any mistakes was huge. I wanted to do Leanne proud. I didn't want to let our family down. As I put on my lipstick, I prayed to God to help me hold it together enough to be articulate.

Poor Anthony was really struggling. I watched him for a full ten minutes trying to do up his belt, but he couldn't because his hands were shaking so much. I found myself laughing, which made him worse. I fell off the bed, I was laughing so much, and the more I did, the more annoyed he got.

'This has to stop!' he said. 'You keep saying yes to these things and we've no privacy left. We're not doing it any more!'

'Come here, boy,' I said, getting off the floor. 'I'll tie your belt for you.'

'Get away from me! I'm well able to tie my own belt!'

In the end I helped him, still laughing. It took my mind off what was ahead.

At TV3, the make-up girl didn't have to do any work on me. Anthony got some powder on his face, which was a new one for him. My nerves were back a million times over when I sat down on the set during a commercial break, opposite presenter Mark Cagney. I knew him already, because his sister worked with me and she was a good buddy, but it was like I'd never seen the man before. I'd say I looked to him like a deer caught in the headlights.

The minute the interview started, though, my fear

disappeared. It was like everything melted away around me and I was on my own, answering the questions. I had the comfort of knowing that Anthony was beside me, but if I put my leg too near to his, I'd feel him shaking. He was still a bag of nerves.

At the beginning, when I first went on Neil Prendeville's radio show, I was talking as the grief-stricken mother of a daughter who committed suicide. In the RTÉ radio documentary, Anthony and I were going over what we'd learned from Leanne's diaries about how she battled with all those bullies. But on *Ireland AM* that morning, I was there with a new purpose bubbling under the surface.

As I had before, I told the story of Leanne's suicide and how we found out about it, how Triona discovered the diaries under her bed the day of the funeral, and then Mark Cagney talked about the 'litany of five years of torment' contained within them.

'There was name-calling, there was abuse,' he said. 'She was beaten up, not just beaten up a couple of times, but regularly – it was like it was a hobby for some of these people. Car vandalised ... There was a text campaign . . . She had been knocked unconscious. She had bald patches from her hair being pulled out on a regular basis . . .'

As he said it, it was like hearing it again for the first time, the bullying she'd had to endure, the pain she went through.

'There's a very famous saying, "All that is required for evil to succeed is for good men and women to do nothing,"' Mark said, as the interview came to a close, and he left the last word to me.

'My message is to children out there that are being bullied, and their parents, mainly their parents, we thought it was hormones with Leanne when she'd come in and she was moody and upset ...' For the first time I found myself not able to say what I needed to say. Mark, who has children himself, saw that I was struggling and rescued me. 'As a parent all you can say to them is that there's nothing so bad that you can't tell us.'

'Don't bottle it up,' Anthony added.

I knew from previously telling Leanne's story in the media that it had an impact. People came up to me on the street in Cork to say they'd heard me and they'd tell me of suicides in their own families. Complete strangers told me their stories of heartbreak, pain and guilt. It was like letting out something so many were holding in. In talking about the taboo subject of suicide, I helped give other people the courage to speak about it to me.

I had no idea, however, what the enormous impact of appearing on national television would be, the shift from talking only about Leanne's torment and suicide to acknowledging that bullying was a big issue for young people everywhere. In doing that, we were tapping into something even bigger.

I'd prayed for meaning in Leanne's death. God's answer was that I must find a way to help young people who were being bullied. My first chance would come before I knew it.

38

I know that it gives many people comfort to visit their loved ones' graves, but I've never liked doing it. The idea of talking to the people I've lost as they lie six feet under doesn't sit right with me. Instead of taking consolation from being near them, the awfulness of their funerals comes back to me. I'm horrified again that they've gone into a hole in the ground. It was the same with Leanne. It didn't give me any solace to spend time at her graveside.

Still, Anthony and I visited it to clean it up and put new flowers out. It was a thing we could do as parents that was like continuing to take care of her. It was painful rather than comforting, but in some way it was like an anchor. Tending her grave was something to hold on to.

One day we arrived home from a visit to the graveyard. When we pulled into our house I noticed a jeep parked on the other side of the street with some people sitting inside. The driver, a man in his fifties, looked at me as I opened the front door, but didn't make any gesture to say hello.

Once inside, I inched the net curtains on the front window aside to see if the jeep was still there. 'I think they're here to see us,' I said to Anthony.

I watched as he went out to say hello, the man winding his window down to talk. Then, after a few exchanged words, three people got out of the car, two parents and a young girl of about fifteen. Even from a distance I could see the girl was beautiful. She had black hair tied back and no make-up, but her face didn't need it. She was model material.

Her name was Hazel. She sat on our sofa staring at the floor as her parents, furnished with tea and biscuits, told us her story. They lived in a small town in Clare and had driven all the way to Cork, having gotten our address from Sinéad, one of the researchers for *Ireland AM*. Hazel, one of two children, had always been good at school and happy, but in the last few years she'd been the victim of vicious bullying, both in the playground and in the town. Hair had been torn from her head, earrings ripped from her ears. Like Leanne, she was being bullied online and by text too.

Her father, a big, well-dressed man, who you'd think would be able to handle just about anything, almost broke down as he told us that he'd been arrested after going to tackle Hazel's bullies. He knew the police had done it for his own protection, to defuse the situation, but he was at his wits' end. He and his wife had seen me on *Ireland AM* and they didn't know where else to turn. They were desperate. Hazel had told them she wanted to take her own life.

That poor young girl's eyes met mine for a second and in them I saw terrible sadness. I saw resignation too, as if there was nothing that could be done and she'd given up. But she *had* done something. She had told her parents about what was happening and they'd had a chance to help her. They'd fought for her, they'd talked to her, and they'd ended up driving her all the way to Cork to see me. If Leanne had only told me what was happening to her, if she'd mentioned she felt suicidal, I would have gone to the ends of the earth to help her. I would have done what these parents were doing. I would have saved her.

'Do you mind if I talk to you alone?' I asked Hazel.

She shook her head. Her parents quietly left the room to sit with Anthony in the kitchen and I took a seat on the sofa beside her.

'I think you have a little play going on in your head,'

I said, as gently as I could. 'You'll kill yourself and those bullies will be sorry for what they did. You'll have a beautiful funeral and there will be flowers and music, and people will remember you as a lovely person, not the girl those bullies say horrible things about. But that's not what happens. The bullies get to live and you don't. You're not there for the funeral, you don't get to see any of it. But your mam and dad and your brother will be there, and their lives will be destroyed. They will never get over it, so the bullies will have won with them too.'

I took her up to Leanne's room, which I'd left exactly the way it was when she died, only tidier because myself and Triona couldn't stop ourselves cleaning it. I pulled the box from under the bed.

'These are my daughter's diaries,' I said. 'That's all we have of Leanne now. A box of sad stories.'

Hazel took one of the diaries in her hands. I could see she wanted to open it and read.

'Life is meant to be lived, girl,' I said. 'We all go through bad times, we all meet bad people along the way, but there are good times too, and good people. You have your mother and your father. You have your good friends and your brother. They will be the people you can lean on, who will help you. And one day, when you're grown-up, you can help them in return. That's the way life is. It's about love, not hate. It's about taking care of each other.'

'They're never going to leave me alone,' she said. They were the first words out of her mouth since she walked into the house.

'You will grow up,' I said. 'And when you do, those bullies will mean nothing to you. You just have to do your best to close your mind to them, to not let them inside. You have your whole life ahead of you, girl. Don't let them take that away.'

I'd love to say that all was well with Hazel after her parents brought her to our house that day, but it wasn't. The bullying went on and intensified, and no authorities could do anything about it. Hazel's parents had to be on watch 24/7 in case she tried to commit suicide. I kept in touch with her by text to see what was going on, trying to encourage her from afar to stay strong, to keep talking to her mam and dad about her feelings.

A year later Anthony and I were asked to go on the TV show *Would You Believe?* to talk about Leanne's death and our subsequent journey with God. The crew came down from Dublin to film in Cork, and on the last day of the shoot we were in the graveyard. The producer, Stephen Plunkett, was a lovely man. We were walking away from Leanne's headstone, when he said to Anthony and me, 'We'll have to get your bank details so we can pay you for doing this.'

'No way,' I said. 'That won't be happening.' I felt like it would be taking something from my daughter's death.

Anthony agreed. 'I'm telling you straight out,' he said, 'we couldn't touch money like that.'

But the producer said, 'You don't understand, Collette. RTÉ has enough money and they are contracted to pay you for doing this. You're helping people with your story.'

A thought came into my head. 'I don't know if this would be possible,' I said, 'but we know this young girl in Clare who is really struggling with horrific bullying. Would you bring your cameras up to her school, and to the local garda station, and see what they're doing about it? Put them on the spot, like?'

Stephen took this in and nodded, as if he was agreeing to my plan.

'And can you use the money you were going to pay us for counselling for her?'

I didn't hear anything more from Stephen after that. I didn't have the courage to ask Hazel if my request had been granted.

A few years later, Hazel came to see me. She stayed over in our house and chatted late into the night. The bullying hadn't stopped so she'd left school before doing the Leaving and studied to be a hairdresser. She wasn't the same sad little thing that had sat silently on my couch the day I first met her. I could see a spark in those eyes now.

'Can I ask you something?' I said. 'Did you ever hear from the RTÉ *Would You Believe?* people?'

Hazel smiled. 'I still get counselling, Collette,' she said. 'I'm brought to Dublin once a week for it.'

I was blown away. Stephen had taken my request seriously. The cameras had gone to Hazel's school. It had frightened the authorities into trying hard to do something, but in truth Hazel was never going to get away from her bullies as long as she was there.

'I have a boyfriend now, Collette,' Hazel said, seeming very grown-up all of a sudden. 'We're going on holidays together.'

As I told her how delighted I was for her, I thought, *Leanne was a part of this. Leanne's story helped this girl.*

I remembered sitting on Leanne's bed that day with Hazel as she opened the diary to read, and thinking about how many Hazels were out there, how many Leannes, how many young boys, all being bullied, all thinking their lives weren't worth it any more.

I didn't know it then, but God was showing me how He was going to use me. Before He uses you, though, He has to heal you. That wasn't going to be an easy ride.

39

Anthony and I continued going to church. We both read the Bible every day and took what comfort we could from God's word, but after a while we felt a piece of the puzzle was missing. At first, I couldn't put my finger on it. I knew I was being told there was something else we had to reach for, but I couldn't figure out what that was. After a while, our visits to church tapered off. The focus there seemed to be about asking God for things and increasingly I felt uncomfortable with that.

We'd always been about things, Anthony and I, buying this or that, getting new cars and gadgets, presents for the children, filling our lives with possessions. I never knew what contentment was. I used to lie in bed and daydream that I'd won a thousand euro, imagining all the things I could do with it. By the end of the dream, ten million wouldn't have been enough for what I wanted.

Leanne's death made all our possessions worse than meaningless. They were something we'd used to make ourselves feel better about who we were, about our standing in the world. But having those things hadn't made a blind bit of difference when it came to Leanne's death. We could have won the lotto and our child would still have kept the secrets that sent her to her grave. And after her death, I only wanted her back, not a new car or the latest television. No material belonging could fill the gap she left behind.

We didn't go to any church services for a while, but without that focus I worried that we were slipping backwards. I didn't want to go back to the Catholic Church I'd been brought up in. Although there are many good clergy, all I could see when I thought of Catholicism were the nuns at my school when I was a child and the disregard they had for my education.

I decided there had to be other options so I went where everyone goes when they want to find something, these days – Google. My search results immediately came up with a place called Redeemed Christian Church of God, Inspiration House, Cork, a Christian church west of Cork City. I clicked on the site and found there was a prayer meeting the following evening.

'We're going,' I told Anthony. He knew better than to argue.

The Inspiration House prayer meeting was in a room on the first floor of a building just off the Kinsale roundabout. When we arrived, both of us were very nervous. We didn't know if we'd be welcome.

A lady was making her way down the stairs as we were going up. She stopped and shook our hands enthusiastically, as if she'd been expecting us. In the prayer room there were only men and they were all black. Anthony and I hesitated. In our previous church there were those of every race and everyone mixed well. But here I was worried we might be the only white people and that we wouldn't fit in.

One of the men stood up. He had a beautiful open face and a smile that almost shouted, 'Welcome!' As we would learn, this was Pastor Paul Orimolusi, the pastor of Inspiration House, Cork. The woman who met us on the stairs was his wife, Hope. We told Pastor Paul our names and he introduced us to the people present as if we were old friends of his.

From that moment I knew there was something special about that church. The people there had the same kind of spirit as us. Their relationship with God was about helping. It was about being there for other people, no matter who they were, Christian or not. It was about showing compassion and love to those who felt unloved or who were in need. It was about acts of kindness.

Although I didn't really know it at the time, I was drawn to the kindness I found in Inspiration House because it was the very opposite to what had driven my daughter to take her own life. It was the opposite of the anger and hatred that she experienced and felt towards her bullies.

It was the opposite of the anger and hatred I still felt for those people. I had this kernel of peace inside me, but I didn't want to let my anger go. It burned like a fire that would never damp down. I didn't show it to anybody, but my rage was capable of murder. It was capable of torture. And it felt righteous, like something I could grab on to. It seemed to help me make some sense of Leanne's death, even though there was no sense to be made of it at all. I joined Inspiration House because it was about love and kindness, but I could find no love or kindness in my heart for Leanne's bullies. I didn't pray for them. I didn't pray for my anger to go. I didn't pray for God's help to forgive them.

Instead, I began to study the Bible more closely. I'd been told I was stupid as a child, and for my whole life I'd believed that was true. But now I started realising that God was bringing something out in me: I could understand things more. Whereas I once couldn't read a sentence, I was taking step after step in reading whole passages, whole pages. As I looked deeper into God's word, I felt I was understanding things that professors wouldn't get to grips with.

I liked Pastor Paul. At the beginning I was cagey, not sure how much to tell him, but slowly I began to open up to him about my life. He listened intently and was able to use the Bible to give me guidance.

At the Inspiration House church services the strangest thing began to happen. I started to feel moments of pure joy in God's presence, which were different from what I'd experienced before. They didn't come laced with guilt. I could feel happiness without battling against myself because Leanne had taken her life. I could feel God's love in my heart without judgement.

I didn't pray to forgive Leanne's bullies. I didn't pray for my own healing. Ever since my appearance on *Ireland AM*, and the subsequent visit from Hazel and her parents, there was something I knew I wanted to do.

The apostle Peter was a fisherman who had no education, but he became a teacher. He became an inspiration for good in the world. I had no education. The idea of speaking in public made me feel sick with terror, but my prayers were all about doing this. I wanted to educate young people about bullying and the impact of suicide. I wanted to hit them while they were young so that they would be clued in about the choices they made as they went through their teenage years.

I didn't know how on earth that was going to happen, but I didn't worry about it. I knew that if this was God's purpose for me, He would find a way for it to be done.

40

I'm well able to leave my prayers in God's hands nowadays, but back then I felt I needed to be all action. I worried that if I didn't do something about speaking to young people, it might not happen at all. But how was I to go about it? Could I just walk into a school and ask a principal? My past experience, going to Leanne's school about her bullying, didn't fill me with confidence.

Anthony said I should take Pastor Paul's advice. I should just pray on it and wait for God to work out the logistics. I did my best, but I had a bee in my bonnet. I'd been asked back to *Ireland AM* a couple more times to talk about bullying and suicide. Maybe I could put out an appeal the next time I was on the show, telling schools I was available.

It turned out Pastor Paul was right. I didn't have to take any action at all.

One day Anthony was tapping away at his laptop across the table from me, when he started laughing.

'I think your prayers have been answered, Collette,' he said.

An email from a man called Mick Finn, a counsellor at Deerpark School in Cork, had arrived. He wanted to know if I'd come in and talk to the boys.

It felt like being handed a big, juicy slice of chocolate cake. 'Tell him yes,' I said, without hesitation.

When it came to the day itself, I was all hesitation. Listening to the noise of the boys as they sat down in the massive hall, I couldn't believe I'd gotten myself into this. How could I, a woman who had left school in her early teens, not even able to read and write, expect to stand up in front of three hundred young Einsteins and educate *them*? I must have been out of my mind, praying to God for such an eventuality.

When Anthony and I arrived at the school that morning, Mick Finn brought us into his office for a chat. 'Collette,' he said, 'you'll be talking to the sixth years today. There'll barely be a boy there who doesn't have some sort of problem going on in his life. There could have been suicide in their homes, or broken marriages, depression, alcoholism, drugs ...' He went through a long list.

'No pressure, then.' I laughed, although my stomach was on the floor.

'Just be yourself and tell the truth,' Mick said. 'You'll be fine.'

I'd brought a photo of Leanne to show the boys, and as I started my talk, it helped with the rush of nerves. I felt I had her with me.

'This is my daughter, Leanne,' I said, to the assembled boys, holding the photograph up, and then, in the same way as it had when I was first on *Ireland AM*, everything around me seemed to melt away.

'She was an ordinary girl. She didn't have two heads, or three ears, or two noses. She was in sixth year, like yourselves, and she was planning to study to be a midwife ...'

I had no notes with me. I told the whole story from my heart, the devastation of her loss, and I could feel the energy in the room rising. The boys were listening so intently you could have heard a pin drop. Some of them were crying.

I had a thought. *I should bring these children into it. I should make it about them, not just Leanne.*

I pointed to a boy in the front row. 'You could call the fella sitting beside you a name today and think nothing of it,' I told him. 'But he could have been called twenty horrible names before he came out the door of his house this morning, or out on the street. The name you call him could push him over the edge. It could make him think, *What's the point of even trying any more?*

'You might all think bullying is kicking someone or beating them, but my daughter wrote in her diary that the worst thing was the name-calling. She could deal with the bruises, but it was words that killed her in the end. You shame someone when you call them names, and shame is harder than a beating, because when you carry shame it paralyses you. It feels like the world is against you and you live in fear.

'We're all different shapes and sizes. Some wear glasses, some don't. Some have problems with weight, some don't. But most people are battling with something. Leanne lost her auntie, who was like a second mother to her, so there was a chip in her armour. She was vulnerable, so when she was told that she was ugly and fat, she didn't have the defences not to let it in.

'You never know what's going on in another person's life. No one knew what was going on with Leanne, not even her parents. I thought she was a young, happy, vibrant teenager and that the world was her oyster. But she was living in a secret Hell.

'Don't for one minute think that your actions have no consequences. If you are horrible to someone, it can go as far as destroying lives. The consequence of bullying for my daughter was her death. The consequences for me, her mother, for her father, her brother and sister are more painful than you can ever imagine.

'But there are consequences if you are kind to someone too. You get to have a positive impact on that person's life. You get to be someone who is doing good in the world. Which would you prefer to live with yourself? The consequences of kindness or the consequences of cruelty?'

When it was over, Anthony and I couldn't get out of the place quick enough, we were so nervous. I was full of doubt over whether I'd done well or not. It was a couple of years later before I bumped into Mick Finn on the street.

'The impact was huge,' he told me. 'It went all through the school. There was a real sense of the boys respecting each other.'

After I spoke at Deerpark, another school got in contact, looking for me to come in, and another one. In the years since then, I've been all over the country talking to young people. I don't think there's anything stronger than someone standing there, face to face, telling young people that their child took her own life because of bullying. I think it has a much more meaningful influence than picking up leaflets and reading some information.

My sister works in a supermarket. One day she was on the till and a young girl came up to her. She said she'd heard me talk. 'I was a bit of a bully myself,' she told my sister. 'But I'm changing my ways.'

I believe these kinds of talks should be done annually with the first-years who are just coming in to secondary. The new ones need to be shown that there is a better way of treating each other, and what the impact of bullying can be.

There are still many schools in Ireland that I haven't visited. Sometimes, I think principals are in denial. They like to think that bullying is not going on, and if they acknowledge that it is, they're worried about opening up a can of worms. Some feel that talking about suicide to kids is bringing it on, rather than discouraging it. But I speak to a lot of young people and I never fail to be shocked by how many want to end their lives. It shouldn't be the elephant in the room any more: suicidal tendencies in our young people should be out in the open. Talking about it is the only way we're going to tackle it.

Certain schools ask me back again and again because they're trying to do things differently. They're trying to have a conversation. They're trying to stem the tide of bullying and suicide by saying there is always someone you can talk to.

For lots of people over the years I have become that person. People in dire straits seek me out in Marks & Spencer. Sometimes I might just be serving a customer and all of a sudden they'll have an emotional collapse in front of me.

When I talk to these customers, or to the children in the schools, or the people who come up to me on the street, I always have compassion in my heart. This is the gift God has given me. I hold all this love for Leanne. I can't give it to her any more, but I can give it to other people. Their problems are never too big. For the time I'm with them, I can help carry their burden, as I hand them over to God..

I won't lie, there are some people I run a mile from, the ones who are living it up at a pity party. These people would suck you dry if you let them. I recognise them quickly and move on. But there are many people out there who are genuine and struggling, with their backs against the wall. God gives me the grace to be of service to them.

At Deerpark School that first day, I spoke to the boys about kindness. In my dealings with people I came into contact with, I held love and compassion in my heart, but beneath it the fire of my hatred for Leanne's bullies was still burning bright. Earlier on in this book, I wrote that there was a price to be paid for walking with God. Slowly I came to learn that my price was forgiveness, not only of the bullies who made my daughter's life a living hell but of the man who'd destroyed my childhood. I just didn't know where to start.

47

I remember the moment when God put forgiveness front and centre in my healing journey. I was reading in the Bible about Jesus on the cross and the words He cried to the heavens jumped out at me: 'Forgive them, Father, for they know not what they do.'

I had read many times about Jesus in the worst of His suffering, naked, bleeding and crucified, asking God to forgive His tormentors, but suddenly I knew these words were a call to action for me. When I realised it, I thought, *This is me and God parting company.* I could forgive my sexual abuser quicker than I could Leanne's bullies.

In my imagination I had spent long days tearing them apart with my bare hands. I wanted them to live in abject misery. I wanted their families to have untold suffering. I wanted these people to pay the price of their own lives for what they had done to my daughter. I prayed every night that a truck would roll over them, or a plane would land out of the sky on top of them. The mere mention of their names got my stomach churning with rage. How could I forgive people I literally hated?

A few days after I read Jesus's cry from the cross, Mark Ryan made one of his regular house calls. We were sitting with a cup of coffee when I started crying.

'I think God is asking me to forgive Leanne's bullies,' I told him. 'But there's no way I can do it.'

I thought that God would leave me, that He'd say I wasn't good enough because I couldn't forgive. I knew I couldn't lie and say I forgave them, because He would know what was in my heart.

'Will God forgive me for not forgiving them?' I asked Mark.

Mark gave me a kind smile. 'Don't think about it too much,' he said. 'If and when you're ready, just ask and God will find a way to give you the grace to forgive.'

I didn't think I'd ever be ready. But I kept imagining God saying to me, 'How much do you love me, Collette? Enough to forgive them?' It was like an equation: I couldn't really love God unless there was forgiveness in my heart.

I took it up with Pastor Paul. He showed me scriptures about loving your enemies, those who persecute you.

'I don't care about them persecuting me,' I said. 'It's what they did to my child.'

Again I was told to be patient, to ask and I would receive. But I couldn't bring myself to ask.

I prayed and prayed, not to find a way to ask, but to help me deal with the rage I felt inside. It was like a cancer eating away at the peace I had otherwise found.

One evening Anthony and I were at Bible study. The subject we were discussing was internal anger and how God might help you face it.

I looked at my husband and wondered what he was thinking, whether he still felt the same fury with Leanne's tormentors as I did. I hadn't shared my murderous thoughts with him because I worried it would be like lighting the fuse on a bomb. I could still remember the night he had filled his van with implements to kill those people.

I put my hand up. The discussion stopped and everybody turned to me. I could see them wondering, *What's she going to come out with?*

'I need help,' I said. 'I need you to pray for me. I have terrible anger – it's consuming me. I get it under control, but then it comes rushing in again and it feels like I'm drowning in hate.'

The room set up to praying for me, Anthony too. I could see in his eyes that he knew what I was feeling, that he wanted to help me. I knew that in helping me, he would be helping himself.

The words 'Forgive them, Father, for they know not what they do' came back to me, and I knew what I must do.

I had to pray for them, that God would heal them from the pain that had brought them to the place where they would do such things as they had done to Leanne. I had prayed hard for their lives to be full of suffering, but they must have already been miserable to make somebody else feel like that. Leanne was loved, cherished and adored, but I don't think that those young girls at the time ever felt that or knew how important they were.

I won't lie, it was not easy to pray for them. But I did it. I asked God to help them find a way to end their suffering. I knew that every time I spoke in the media, every time Leanne's photograph appeared in a newspaper, it brought back the things they'd done. They could never be free of Leanne's suicide, not only because I'd fought so publicly for it not to be in vain, but because they never thought their actions would end in this place, that they'd be forever tarnished with the fact that they had driven a young, innocent girl to the point of killing herself. I knew each of them would go to their deathbeds with this burden. So I prayed they might acknowledge their actions, make amends for them in some way, and know peace.

It can only be God's grace to forgive them in the end. If they stand in front of me, I want them to know that I hope they're going to make better lives than they've made already. I hope they're kinder and that they learn to treat people with a bit more respect. I hope they can say, 'All right, we did wrong. We can't change this, because Leanne's gone, but we can make it better for other people.'

They can make a difference in their families' lives, their children's lives. They can be better people. I pray that one day I might meet Leanne's main bully and that I will see a change in her. I hope she gets a touch from God, that He gives her the freedom not to make other people's lives a misery.

Forgiveness does not come easy, and it doesn't come all at once. It's simple but very complicated at the same time. Sometimes I slip back a few steps and feel a bit of my old anger. Sometimes I worry that my children won't understand that I have forgiven, because they're not there yet.

Forgiving my abuser was straightforward compared to the journey I had with Leanne's bullies. The strange thing about sexual abuse is that sometimes children love their abusers. In my case it's not about love, but the feeling I have isn't hatred. I never hated him. I was always afraid of him and felt very vulnerable around him, but I didn't want to exact any revenge. With hindsight, I know that this is because I took on the responsibility for my abuse. I felt the shame rather than putting it on him.

The past is gone. My secret is out and I'm not ashamed any more. Maybe in allowing God to hold me, rather than feeling I have to hold all these things alone, I've set myself free from my abuser.

When I think about that little eight-year-old girl now, I'd like to say to her, 'You will grow up to be a strong woman who knows the difference between right and wrong, a woman who can find it in her heart to love everyone rather than hate anyone. One day you will find it in your heart to forgive this man and move on.'

Telling the woman who found her daughter's diaries on the morning of her funeral that one day she will move on from the bullying contained in those pages is a different thing altogether. Before that could happen I would have to face going back to the last locality I ever wanted to visit, the scene where much of Leanne's abuse took place.

42

I don't know exactly when God dropped the idea into my heart that I'd go on *The Late Late Show*, but I can tell you it was a long time before the actual event happened. I had told my husband and family that it would be happening.

'Good luck with that one,' Anthony said. 'I won't be with you.'

As fearful as he was of going on *Ireland AM*, *The Late Late Show* has a live audience. The thought of it terrified him.

When, some time later, we did get a call from *The Late Late Show*'s producers, I persuaded Anthony to do it with me. I knew I wouldn't be able to go on alone. We went to stay in Dublin for the night of the show, and when the taxi arrived at our hotel to pick us up at the arranged time, the tension between us was unreal.

'I can't believe you've talked me into doing this,' Anthony complained. 'After this, you're on your own.'

As we got into the taxi, there was an awful awkward silence between us. The driver said, 'So, you're on *The Late Late* tonight?'

'We are,' I said, glancing at Anthony's fuming face. 'We've come up from Cork.'

'Is that right?' the taxi driver said. 'What are you on to talk about?'

'I won twenty-five million in the lotto,' I said. 'And I'm still working in Marks & Spencer's.'

I knew that if I had spoken about why we were on, about Leanne, Anthony would have jumped out of the taxi and run all the way home to Cork. I needed to break the ice.

'Twenty-five million and you're not giving up your job!' The taxi man couldn't believe his ears.

'That's right,' I said. 'I absolutely love my job.'

Out of the corner of my eye, I could see Anthony had cracked the tiniest smile.

Just a few minutes before we got to RTÉ, I said to the driver, 'I was only kidding about the lotto. We're really going on because we lost our daughter to suicide.'

The driver caught my gaze in his rear-view mirror.

'My sympathies are with you,' he said. 'I almost lost my son to the same.'

No matter who you talk to about suicide, there's nobody untouched by it. That's why I had agreed to do the interview in the first place. When the researcher for the show first contacted me, I was very clear about what I wanted to say. I'd never directly asked for anything before when I was interviewed, but I knew that the whole country would be watching this show.

'Before we agree, I have something to tell you,' I said. 'I know you want to hear all the gory details about Leanne's suicide and our grief, but I won't be going on unless we're able to give people some hope. I'm not doing this for me. I'm doing it for the ones who think there is no hope. They'll hear our story and think there's no recovering for people who have experienced the loss we have. But when the penny drops that we have found hope, maybe they'll think it's possible for them too.'

The researcher came back after talking to the producers and said, 'Yes, Collette, you will be given an opportunity to speak about hope.'

By the time we were brought down to the studio and about to go on, Anthony had calmed down a bit. He'd eaten half the snack bar in the green room to steady his nerves. But then someone tilted the massive black curtain in front of us a little bit.

'Who are they?' Anthony said, when we saw the

rows of faces behind it. The colour had drained from his face.

They were the live audience, of course. We knew they were going to be there, but it's nothing like you see on the telly. You feel there's hundreds of them, row after row, all expectantly waiting for you.

There were about five people standing around us at the side, the researcher and some cameramen.

'I need to talk to my husband for a second,' I said, to no one in particular.

I took Anthony's hand in mine and said, 'Lord, I'm asking you to strengthen us. We have no strength of our own. Help us. Let it be that the world will know that there is hope, in Jesus's name.'

One of the cameramen was staring at us and I could actually read the thought that was in his head: *What a pair of weirdos*.

Then Ryan Tubridy appeared at our side. The first thing he said was, 'My goodness!' He was taking in my hair and make-up, which I'd had professionally done in Cork that morning.

'Would you like to walk on when I introduce you, or would you prefer to be already sitting down, during a commercial break?' he asked.

'Commercial break,' I replied, my throat closing. My legs wouldn't have been able to walk onto that set after he'd introduced us, so we took our seats while the ads were on and sat there with the entire audience staring at us in silence.

Ryan is a good interviewer. I could really feel him empathising with our story, and in turn the audience seemed to be very moved. But the time flew by and suddenly we were coming to the end of Leanne's story without me getting to say anything at all about hope.

'Thank you for coming on and telling us your story,' Ryan said, wrapping the whole thing up.

I was thinking, *This is not going to happen. We're not ending this with the poor, sorrowful Collette and Anthony just sitting here.*

'Before I go, I need to tell people there is hope,' I blurted out.

Ryan looked a little taken aback, but he said, 'Go ahead.'

'You can come through this,' I continued. 'Tonight, if anything, don't feel sorry for us. We have a wonderful life, and I'll see my daughter again one day, with the grace of God. We have hope now in our life, and we do a daily walk. We are in a good place. Thank you.'

All the responses to the show afterwards were about hope. In those few seconds we touched a chord. Everywhere we went in Dublin the next day, people came up to tell us they were moved by our hope in the face of such loss. There was even a crowd of teenagers in Starbucks who sat down to talk to us.

The morning after our appearance, Anthony was worried. 'We didn't say a lot about God,' he said.

I wasn't concerned. I'd left the whole thing in God's hands, knowing something would come from it, whether for a lot of people or just one.

It turned out that, among the hundreds of thousands looking at *The Late Late Show* that night, there was one young girl who was in terrible trouble. She would be the catalyst who brought us back to the place where Leanne suffered most.

43

The day I got the call to go to Mayfield, I knew that God was on the line. A woman there had seen me on *The Late Late Show* and she wanted me to come to her house to talk to a few people she knew from the estate who were in difficulty, with various trials and tribulations.

My first response was resistance. I did not want to go back to Mayfield. It was the place where Frances and I had had so many happy times before she died. It was the place where my daughter had experienced the worst of her torment, where I had found her surrounded by a gang of screaming bullies who had vandalised her car just weeks before she took her own life.

I told Anthony about the woman's request and he said we should go, but still I was resistant. I prayed to know the right thing to do, and the answer came loud and clear: God was using the woman to call me back to Mayfield for some reason I didn't understand yet.

I still felt very uncomfortable about it, so I asked Pastor Paul to come with us. He wasn't familiar with the estate, and when we arrived he parked in the exact spot where Leanne's car had been vandalised. He noticed immediately that something was wrong.

'Are you all right, Collette?' he asked.

'I'm fine,' I told him, but there were tears pouring out of my eyes.

'You're not fine, sister,' he said. 'Tell me what's in your heart.'

'To be honest, I don't find Mayfield an easy area to come to,' I told him. 'Leanne was bullied here. She wrote a lot about it in her diaries.'

Somehow, telling him about my feelings made them easier to manage. 'We're here for a reason,' Pastor Paul told me. 'God always has an intention.'

The woman's house was packed and they all wanted to talk to myself, Anthony and Pastor Paul individually, and I did my best to take in their stories, but out of the corner of my eye, I kept coming back to a young girl who was standing apart, holding a little boy's hand. I found she couldn't look me in the face, even though I was trying to make contact with her. When I tried to make conversation, she was standoffish.

As we walked out to the car after it was all over, I said to Anthony, 'See all those people in there? We're here for only one of them.'

I knew that God had sent us to that girl.

They started coming to church, this big crowd from Mayfield. They were like a troop that shuffled together as a unit. They reminded me of our family in the wake of Leanne's death, when we all moved as one. The girl was always with them, and her little boy. She began to get a little friendlier, letting her guard down.

Her name was Emma and her son's name was Jimmy. On the odd occasion Emma allowed herself to smile, her whole face lit up, but behind her eyes she was older than her years and there was great sorrow there. You can't hand anyone else peace, but you can find ways to be there for a person you know really needs you. Mark Ryan did that with us, coming to our house all those nights, talking with us, listening to us, making sure we were okay. That's what we did with Emma.

She kept coming back to church, even after some of the Mayfield crowd had dispersed. I began to collect her for services and feed her a bit of dinner afterwards. She remained quiet, accepting my help but not saying much other than 'thank you'. There was a sense that she was running from something.

As time went on, I started asking her mother to come for dinner with her. I didn't want to exclude Emma's family, for them to be thinking I was taking her over. I found her mam friendly and easy to talk to.

Emma was due to come over for church and dinner one Sunday, when I said, 'Do you and Jimmy want to stay the night?'

She said they would. On the day itself, we brought her out to the shops to pick new nightclothes for herself and her little boy. They started staying regularly. They'd come on Friday, stay on Saturday, go to church on Sunday, and then we'd drop them home.

One weekend we were sitting down to dinner after Jimmy had gone to sleep. We'd just finished grace, when I said, 'Emma, can I ask you something? Why was God in such a hurry to bring us to Mayfield for you?'

She put her fork down. 'I don't want to discuss it, Collette,' she said, looking at her plate.

I felt a surge of love for this girl who was so caught up in pain that she thought she couldn't share it. I remembered my own teenage girl and the pain she couldn't share. 'You know me well enough by now to know that's not going to wash,' I said. 'Come on, I need to know.'

It was at least a minute before she spoke. 'Before I met you I had decided to end my life,' she said. I could see it was taking all her effort to get the words out.

She began to cry. She's not a girl who cries easily, and in that way she reminds me of Leanne a bit. That's probably why I feel a special bond with her. She's not Leanne, there's no teenager who can come into my life and take my daughter's spot, but some of Emma's ways remind me of her. She reminds me of myself too, because she'd grown up living behind a mask.

People thought she had a nice home life, because she presented it that way, but in fact she faced many challenges in her home life, and she did her best to raise her little boy, without his father in the picture, in difficult circumstances.

She'd come to the house in Mayfield that evening because she'd seen me on *The Late Late Show*. She'd seen me talk about hope and wondered could we lie about something like that. 'I knew that you loved your daughter,' she said. 'I knew you would never have let the things happen to her that did if you had known. And when you said you had found hope through the grace of God, I was thinking, *Maybe God is real*.'

I once thought my calling was to work at Marks & Spencer. But my real calling was to let the world know what God can do. I want to shout it from the rooftops. I know loneliness and despair, I know what it's like to be bereft of hope, and I know that when I'm talking there could be just one person listening who will take a chance with God, who will have come to the point where they need Him in their lives.

Emma said she was going to move out of her home, that she was going to go homeless. I told her she could stay with us, but she said she needed to be classified homeless so she could be housed. She and Jimmy went from hotel to hotel, which wasn't easy. I'd collect her, and bring her to the next hotel. Sometimes I'd stay with her in their hotel room, because I knew she needed company. I knew she needed love.

She has a little two-bedroom house now; she's going to college part-time. She still comes to church with Jimmy on Sundays, and now she leads a Bible-study group in my house every week. She still grapples with many things in her life, but she knows, as I know, that God is carrying her. Now the smile that lights up Emma's face seems to be always present.

We made Emma a part of our family, which she is to this day, but I prayed to find a way to help many more people. I wanted to help those who felt life was too hard for them and found themselves on the brink of suicide, and those who had experienced the suicide of others. I wanted to help those who were experiencing or had come through the worst misery. I'd made sure to get my message of hopefulness out on *The Late Late Show*, but I wanted another way to show people the light at the end of the tunnel. It wasn't about recruiting people for church or for God. I knew that God would do that work, and want to guide people towards Him.

After praying for a long time, I got a vision of how I might do it. Unbeknownst to me, Pastor Paul had the same vision.

44

I now realise that all through my life, before Leanne died, I had been hoping for the wrong things. I'd be hoping that Anthony's job would change and we'd have more money, that we'd get a bigger car, a bigger house. All of those things came and they didn't really fill the void that was deep inside. I wanted all sorts of things to fill that void, even my children on some level. When Leanne chose to leave me, all that misdirected hope went with her. But I still didn't know it was misdirected. I thought I would never have what had seemed like hope again.

And then a miracle happened. I was given hope and

it wasn't the kind you'd use to fill a void. It was hope that made me understand life is beautiful, that this world is beautiful and that nothing, not even sexual abuse or rape or suicide, can take away that truth. Hope didn't have to fill a void inside me, because there was no void to be filled any more. God had done that.

I prayed for a way to help other people to find this real hope instead of the misdirected kind, and the vision that came into my head was of hundreds of people together, all with their hands in the air. I was standing among them and we were listening to beautiful music.

I told Pastor Paul about my vision. 'A concert!' he exclaimed. 'That's what I've been thinking of too!'

I don't know who coined the name 'The Concert of Hope' but it came quickly. In fact, from the moment Pastor Paul, Anthony and myself first had the idea, the whole thing came together as if guided by a greater force, which of course it was.

Anthony went to talk to Cork City Council, and he was told we could hold the concert in the Millennium Hall at City Hall, Cork. After that, it was all hands on deck, with our church members at Inspiration House, Cork working together voluntarily. We got an organising committee together and started putting intricate plans in place.

It was not to be a religious concert, except that we knew it was God's plan that we do it and that He'd be in attendance. It was a concert where people who needed hope could come and find it, no matter what their backgrounds were. We decided there would be doctors available, in case first aid was needed, and counsellors for the people who were in need of help.

The first group we asked to perform was the High Hopes choir from Penny Dinners in Cork, a charity that helps feed the homeless and the poor. Many of the users of that service are in great difficulty, but music has lifted their hearts. We knew they were the right people to share a message of hope in dark times. We also asked the Carrigaline Gospel Choir and a few solo singers along.

Anthony contacted the Lord Mayor to open the concert and speak there, and the tradition has continued every year since.

I'd talked to so many media outlets about Leanne's story and now it was payback time. The newspapers wrote about the concert and radio stations advertised it, all free of charge. The very first person to interview me, Neil Prendeville, talked it up on his radio show.

Our slogan was: 'You are not alone. Fear keeps you prisoner, hope sets you free.'

I'm not saying I didn't have any doubts along the road to that first Concert of Hope. Of course I did. I felt like I was taking on something huge, bringing my message to a whole new level, and at the same time I worried that no one would show up. We'd have gone to all this trouble, done all this work, put all this hope into our Concert of Hope, and it would be just us and our church in the Millennium Hall on the big night, looking like fools.

I mentioned my nerves to poor Pastor Paul several times. Well, a lot more than several times, to be honest. He was as cool as a cucumber. 'Don't worry,' he'd say, with that grin of his. 'It's in God's hands.'

I have a photograph that someone took at that first concert. You can just see me from behind, beside Pastor Paul, and we have our hands in the air. Even though you can't see our faces, you know that we're in our heart's desire. I needn't have worried. Hundreds of people turned up. The message had travelled far and wide.

I took an usher's badge and welcomed people as they were coming in. Some I recognised, people who had talked to me on the street about their problems and despair, people who had come up to me in Marks & Spencer. Many I'd never seen before, but they all looked like they could do with hope.

As the choirs sang so beautifully that night, it was wonderful to see all those people with their hands in the air. I could feel the spirit of God moving through the hall and I knew what He was doing. He was sowing the seeds of peace.

Anthony and I went up to the stage to speak, as we have annually since then, in the seven years the Concert of Hope has been going. I didn't know what

I was going to say, I just allowed God to give me the words. 'You are never on your own,' I said to the crowd, after I told them about our journey from Hell to hope. 'People do care about you. Sometimes it might be someone you love, a family member or a friend. Sometimes it might be a complete stranger. But there is love for you. It's all around you in this room tonight. I've experienced it since Leanne left us, and I can tell you, it is everywhere.'

At a Concert of Hope a few years ago, a young woman came up to me and said, 'Collette, do you remember me?'

Everybody thinks you'll remember them, that's human nature, but when you speak to as many people as I do, it's hard to keep everyone in mind.

She had a child by the hand who was about five years old, and she pointed to her. 'We met you at the train station in Carrigtwohill,' she said. 'She was only a tiny baby at the time.'

I remembered them instantly. I'd met the girl one morning as I was waiting for the train to work. Her daughter had been a couple of months old at the time.

She'd told me she was married to a lovely man, but that they were having problems. Her husband, who was Nigerian, wanted her to go to church, but she was reluctant.

'Sure what have you got to lose?' I asked her.

People have this thought when they meet me first: 'Don't be trying to convert me!' Well, nobody can convert anybody. The biggest gift God gave us was free will. Otherwise we'd be like robots – 'Yes, God, no, God, three bags full, God.'

I'd told this girl about Leanne, and about how going to church had helped me. 'Go,' I said to her. 'It might make things better between you and your husband.'

After I'd said goodbye, I realised I hadn't taken her number. I always get a person's number so I can check up on how they're doing, but for some reason I'd forgotten this time. I remember commenting to Anthony about it that night.

It was hectic in the Concert Hall on the evening she said hello again. She told me that things were much better in her marriage and that she was going to church regularly now. I was very busy in the Millennium Hall, so I said, 'Give me your number and I'll call you.'

I gave her a ring the next day and asked would she like to come down for breakfast the following Monday.

Emma came too. When I put their breakfasts in front of them, the girl from the train said, 'I need to say something to you before we go any further.'

She actually looked frightened, so I sat down beside her and said, 'You can tell me anything, girl. We don't judge here.'

'You might want to throw me out of your home,' she said.

'There's always a first.' I laughed, making light of it, but she was crying so I knew it was serious. 'What's so bad that it's bringing you to tears?' I asked. 'I won't throw you out, I promise.'

'You don't know who I am,' she said.

I caught Emma's eye, my brain doing ninety miles an hour.

'Leanne's main bully is my sister,' the girl said.

The silence that descended on the table was so complete, I could hear my own heart thumping.

Her sister was Mary 2, the one who was really violent, who had kicked my daughter and punched her, who had torn out clumps of her hair. She'd hated Leanne for no apparent reason, just going along with the leader of the pack.

All the anger I'd had, all the tormented nights of murderous rage, came back to me, as if they were a movie playing in my head and I was watching it.

Five years previously, when I'd met this girl at the train station, if I had known who she was I would not have been able to talk to her. Now I put my hand on hers. 'I've forgiven your sister,' I said. 'Does that mean I'm ready to have a cup of coffee with her? No. But God hasn't asked me to do that. You did nothing to Leanne. You have done nothing to me and I have nothing against you.'

I looked over at Emma and she was weeping. I began to weep too.

I reached out to give the girl a hug, and we cried together. I thought about how strange it was that this person who was so connected to what had happened to Leanne had appeared in my life, not once but twice. What were the odds?

To this day I have not spoken to any of Leanne's bullies. The thought comes upon me to go and say that I forgive them, but I don't know how that would land. They may not have any guilt or regret, and it could hurt me more than heal me, if they lashed out.

Maybe that day will come, maybe it won't. I'll let God decide. All I know is that having breakfast with the girl, watching her as she recovered herself and chatted to Emma, it felt like the final piece of a puzzle was being put in place. She had been sent to test my forgiveness and show me it was real.

45

A letter written to us by my son, Anthony, the week before his wedding

To Mam, Dad and Triona,
This is my speech for the wedding because it will be too hard on the day to say exactly how I'm feeling. Hopefully this will help me get everything in, because I won't on the day of the speeches.

I just want to start by saying I wouldn't be here if it wasn't for you, Deb and the kids.

Mam, you told me a few times that I was at the lowest

I could go. I know this now because a few days ago I was looking at a few of Leanne's things that I had and I found a letter I wrote a few weeks after she passed away. I don't know who the letter was to and I don't know what it was for, but it went on about the night Leanne died and the phone call I had to make to you.

The screams I heard down the phone that night were the worst I've ever heard and sometimes I woke up to them. In fact it wasn't sometimes, it was a lot.

While my baby sister was upstairs I went outside to tell you, and I must say that was the worst moment of my life. For the first time in my life I didn't have an answer.

I'm going to keep this as positive as possible because I'm not at that point any more. That's because of you and I want to thank you for getting me through a horrible time in my life. You fought for me and I will never forget that.

Sorry for bringing up things about Leanne and I know this should be a happy week, but I just wanted to let you know how I feel and what you got me through.

Everything about my childhood is positive and happy and we couldn't have asked for a better Mam and Dad. The love you gave us is what I try and give to my three boys and if I become half the parent that you were, I'll be a happy man.

Every little problem I had, I'd go to you Mam and you would give me the advice that I needed, no matter how big or small it was. And if you couldn't answer it, you would send me up to Frances, who would have it sorted in two minutes.

As much as I want them days back, I know my job now is to pass on the advice you gave me to my three boys and hopefully my little girl.

Next week is going to be the happiest day of my life, but I can't believe my baby sister won't be there to celebrate it with us. But I do know she will be looking down, smiling and crying and she would want us to have a good day. So, for her we are going to have the best day out that we all deserve.

Your son and brother

My son got married the May bank holiday weekend in 2013. In the intervening years he'd had two more children, Evan and Dillon. Dillon was only a little one-year-old at the wedding, just beginning to crawl. The older ones, Ryan and Evan, were very excited, all dressed up for their mam and dad's celebrations.

It was the first major event for our family since Leanne's death, and in the lead-up to it her absence grew. She loved a big occasion, having her hair done and choosing an outfit, getting a tan and doing her make-up. Being in a crowd appealed to her social side and I'd marvel at the way she worked a room, talking to everyone there, making them all smile and laugh. Six years on from her death it was still hard to imagine that she was not going to be working the room at Ant's wedding, hard to believe that she wouldn't be a bridesmaid, that she wouldn't be at the top table with us, sharing in the celebrations.

Debra had lost her mam two years before Leanne died, so I was the only mother in the picture. But I couldn't do the normal things a mother does. Being around the atmosphere of preparation was too hard to face. Instead, I prayed that we would have a joyful day when it came to it.

Debra and Ant were fourteen and fifteen when they met, and had been joined at the hip since then. They had gone through such a bad time after Leanne's death, both of them, but I could see they were coming into their own once more. Apart from my own loneliness for Leanne, it was lovely to see my son looking forward to his wedding. He was actually laughing and it was so long since I'd heard that laugh.

Anthony and I hadn't been able to help them out financially either. We were still trying to build up that part of our lives. I'd been out of work for a year after Leanne; Anthony had gone back to work, but come out again. Times were still tough, but we didn't mention it to anyone outside the family.

Two days before the wedding, Pastor Paul knocked at the door. When he came in, he handed me an envelope. When I opened it, I saw it was money. I was really taken aback.

'I can't accept that,' I told him.

'God said to give you this gift,' he said. 'So please take it.'

Anthony said, no, we couldn't, but Pastor Paul said

that pride was something we should put aside. He wouldn't listen to any more arguments and he went home, leaving the envelope behind.

It made a huge difference. All of a sudden we were flush! We were able to do all the things parents can do on the day to help Anthony and Deb, and I will be for ever grateful to Pastor Paul and Hope for that.

On the night before the wedding, disaster struck. Deb's father James, who suffered with back problems, was struck down. Ant called me and said, 'He can't get up off the floor. Will you come down, Mam?'

Before I got there, the doctor had arrived and said that James would have to go to hospital. He'd given him an injection to get him up off the floor, but he wanted an ambulance called.

James said, 'Leave me out of hospital for a day so I can see my daughter go to the church. Her mother's not here, so she needs me.'

The doctor reluctantly agreed and said that James would have to go to hospital the minute he'd seen Debra off. He left and I was just about to make my exit too, when a thought came upon me to pray with James. I looked at my son, who was visibly upset that his father-in-law wouldn't be attending the wedding, and thought, *No, I can't do it. They'll all think I've lost my marbles.*

But the urge was strong, so in the end I gave in and got down on my knees.

'James,' I said, 'do you believe in God?'

'I do, Collette.'

'Well, I believe God can heal you.'

My son's eyes were popping out of his head. You could see him thinking, *My mother's really losing it*.

I put my hand on James and said, 'God, I ask you, let this man get up on his feet. Let him dance with his daughter at her wedding. Let tomorrow be a day of joy, not of sadness. In Jesus's name, amen.'

Then I got up said, 'I'm off,' before Ant could tell me I'd lost my mind.

James walked his daughter up the aisle and danced at her wedding. We were in bed before him that night. My son thought I'd worked a miracle, that I'd suddenly become a healer, but I told him it was God who'd done what He could, not me.

The earlier part of the wedding passed in a bit of a blur for me. I remember crying in the church, I was so happy for Anthony and Debra. I remember bringing wine up for the offering. When we sat down at the top table during the reception, Leanne's absence was conspicuous, but we settled into it as best we could.

During the speeches, Ant said, 'Mam, will you say a few words?'

Having told our story so many times, I wasn't afraid of public speaking any more, so I got to my feet without hesitation.

'I welcome Debra into our family. I've loved her

from the minute I met her and I know she and my son will have a good marriage. I ask God to bless their lives together.

'They tell us in the Book of Ecclesiastes that to everything there is a season. Today it is the season to dance and to laugh, and that's what we're going to do. We've done the sorrow. This is a day for joy.'

I look back on that little family at that wedding reception, one of them sorely missing, and think about how much things have changed for us all even since then, how much I've changed.

I was a woman with secrets. My daughter was a teenager with secrets. I don't believe in hiding things now, because the more we hide things, the worse our troubles become. God didn't just create one person: there are seven and a half billion human beings in the world, and we need each other.

I take it daily because, if I look ahead, Leanne is not in that picture, and that's still too hard to think about. Today is a good day. Today I'm not living in sorrow or guilt or shame.

This might shock you to read, and it shocks me to write it. I could not turn back the clock and give God back. It's not an easy thing to say.

God could have saved Leanne on the night. How many other people have been saved who should never have survived? I think she'd had enough, and He said, 'I'll take her home.'

Of course I know this is a thing that any mother of a child who died might say to console herself, and I've grappled with that. Once when I was struggling, I said to Pastor Paul, 'I read in the Bible that nobody should take life. I've researched suicide and it used to be classified as a crime. I don't know how to resolve it in my mind.'

Pastor Paul was quiet for a bit, as he always is when faced with one of my questions. Then he said, 'You know, my sister, God is a merciful God, a God of compassion. One thing we are sure of is that God has brought your family out of darkness and hopelessness, and many lives have been touched positively through your story.'

It was Leanne's time. She fulfilled what she had to fulfil in life. She gave us a wonderful eighteen years and I was very blessed to have that time with her. Some people don't get a week; some people don't get a day. I saw her whole character come out. I saw her become a young woman. Would I have loved to see her go on, to grow older and experience more of what life had to offer? Of course I would. But I can't turn back time.

I don't question why any more. I went through a journey in Hell: it had everything in it – fear, loneliness, doubt, shame, failure, guilt, insecurity, rage, every negative you could imagine and more.

If I could go back to that night in Lanzarote, I would tell that woman who thought her life was over that a different life had just begun.

'You will use Leanne's story to help so many people who are hurting,' I'd tell her. 'From the devastation of this loss will come real hope, not just for you, but for many.'

There will be a time when I stand before God, and when He looks at me, I want Him to say, 'Well done, Collette. You did the best that you could and I'm proud of you.'

I don't carry pain any more. God carries it for me. When people tell me about their pain, I don't carry it either. I pass it on to God, through His son Jesus Christ.

Acknowledgements

To my husband Anthony, for the unending encouragement and love he has shown me on this winding journey we've walked together. To my beloved children Anthony Jnr and Triona, and their wonderful spouses Debra and Edward, for all your love and support. To Mark Ryan, for his courage, patience and love when we most needed it. To Patrycja Stachurka for all her encouragement. To Pastor Paul Orimolusi, who showed me nothing is impossible if you have faith. To all my friends at RCCG Inspiration House, who have been there for us through difficult times, along with my great friends at Marks & Spencer. To my publisher Ciara Considine and everyone at Hachette Ireland, for making this possible. And to Brian Finnegan, for his talent, dedication and sensitivity in telling my story – and for always managing to make me smile.